WRITING BEYOND FEAR
OVERCOME COMMON AUTHOR FEARS AND
WRITE YOUR WAY TO SUCCESS

KATE KRAKE

INKWELL & ELM

Copyright 2024 Kate Krake
All rights reserved.

Inkwell & Elm is an imprint of
Krakenfire Media

ISBN - 978-0-6453181-8-0

The author publisher shall not be held liable or responsible for any loss or damage allegedly arising from any suggestion or information contained in this book. No guarantee or other promise is made as to any results that may be obtained from using the content of this book.
This information in this book does not replace professional medical, psychological, legal, financial, business opinion and advice on any occasion.

Cover Design by Krakenfire Media.
Image attribution:
Fountain Pen Drawing Oval Swirls by aroderick via Adobe Stock
Vector Rainbow by Vitaliy via Adobe Stock

Any administrative inquiries regarding this book should be directed to
Krakenfire Media
admin@krakenfiremedia.com

Statement of AI Use

Generative AI was used to assist in the creation of this book in the following ways:
Spelling and Grammar Check (ProWritingAid)

For all writers who fear something.
Just keep writing.

CONTENTS

Introduction	ix
What Is Fear?	xiii

PART ONE
MINDSET

Being Misunderstood	3
Self-Discipline	5
Losing the Passion	7
Failure	9
Humiliation	12
Someone Finding Out	14
Impostor Syndrome	15
Calling Yourself a Writer	17
Being Overshadowed	18
Irrelevance	19
Existential Uselessness	21
Authority	23
The Unknown	24
Fear	26

PART TWO
CREATIVITY

Unoriginality	29
Writing Something Personal	31
Creative Stagnation	33
Pigeonholing	34
Other Forms of Art	36
Running Out of Ideas	37
Having Too Many Ideas	39

PART THREE
CRAFT

Clichés	43
Short Stories	44
You're Not Skilled Enough for Your Ideas	45
Defining Your Own Book Lengths	47
Defining Your Own Chapter Lengths	48
Bad Prose	49

Word Counts	50
Writing with Multiple Points of View	51
Diversity	53
Writing in a New Genre	54
Elegant Prose	55
Not Writing as Well as We Used To	56

PART FOUR
PROCESS

AI Technology	59
An Unfocused Writing Career	61
Balancing Multiple Writing Projects	63
Failing a Process	64
Inability to Finish a Project	66
Inability to Finish a Series	68
Procrastination	69
Writing and Publishing Technology	71
Research	73
Writing Slow	75
Writing Fast	76
Hard Work	78
Never Writing the Next Book	79
Abandoning a Project	80
Never Finishing	82
Writer's Block	83
First Drafts	84
Low Productivity	86
Wasting Words	88
Experimenting	89

PART FIVE
EDITING

Finding Help	93
Professional Criticism	95
Fixing the First Draft	97

PART SIX
PUBLISHING AND THE WRITING BUSINESS

Authenticity	101
Writing to Market	103
Not Using Social Media	105
Using Social Media	106
Judgment	107

Deadlines	108
External Expectations	110
Not Being Taken Seriously	112
Platform	113
Disorganization	115
Being Compared to Others	117
Losing Creative Control	118
Offending the Subject	120
Offending Readers	122
Controversy	124
Piracy	126
No Money	127
Discoverability	129
Trends	131
Intellectual Theft	133
Rejection	135
Not Selling	137
Negative Feedback	138
The Market	140
Sharing Your Writing	142
Traditional Publishing	143
Independent Publishing	145
Marketing	146
Missing an Opportunity	148
Public Speaking	150
Becoming Obsolete	152

PART SEVEN
LIFESTYLE

It's Too Late	157
It's Too Soon	158
Physical Limitations	160
Isolation and Loneliness	162
Financial Uncertainty	164
Balancing Responsibilities	165
Burnout	167
Writing Conventions	169
Not Having Time to Write	171
Success	173
Qualifications	175
Criticism from Friends and Family	177
Reading	179
Being Devoured by a Flesh-Eating Virus	181

About The Author   185
Also By Kate Krake   187

INTRODUCTION

WRITING IS TERRIFYING

Being a writer is scary.

Writing, particularly creative writing, is subject to rules and standards, guidelines, expectations, and conventions, I believe more so than any other form of artistic expression. Most people can write. A birthday card message, an email, any kind of words on a page to communicate a situation. What's more, many people believe they *could* write a book, if only they had enough time, the right ideas, or any other qualification because they are able to write well in these day to day situations. This puts a lot of pressure on writers that other artists, painters, sculptures, musicians, and the rest, are immune to. It's a pressure from within as much as it is from the outside world. We think, "Anyone who can string a sentence together could do this job. I *should* be able to do this better!"

This pressure creates fear.

All of this fear can paralyze writers. The work suffers. The writer suffers.

Writers not only fear the fact of being read, of baring our

souls on the page for all to see, but we often fear that we might bare our souls wrong in the first place.

Doesn't this seem off?

It's time to release all this pressure, and it's time to release our fears and reclaim all that joyful wonder that being a writer is all about.

WHAT'S THIS BOOK ABOUT?

This book began as an article I wrote on *The Creative Writing Life* (formerly *Three Pillar Authors*). It was a listicle blog post entitled "52 Things a Writer Fears, But Shouldn't." Many authors connected with those fifty-two suggestions and offered their own additions, and in the years and words since writing that post, I've come up against new fears of my own. I write this book from our collective experiences of what it's like to live and work, daring to call ourselves writers.

Here's the TL;DR version of what it's all about.

We do not need to fear writing. We do not need to fear the writing process or the writing business.

Fear is not a bad thing. Sometimes you can overcome it, sometimes you can't. Sometimes you can face the scary feat, feel afraid, and still do it. Fear does not need to stop us from writing; it does not need to stop us from setting goals or striving to reach them. Fear often stems from feeling like we need permission we don't have.

Forget the writing rules, even if it's only momentarily.

Claim whatever permissions you need, or believe you need.

Let other people have their judgments, and know you can choose whether to listen.

Write whatever you want, however you want to write it, and publish it in the ways that feel best to you.

The book is made up of concise chapters, divided into seven themes:

Mindset
Creativity
Craft
Process
Editing
Publishing and the Writing Business
Lifestyle

The sections and chapters are presented in no particular order. You can read them all, beginning to end, or you can skip around to the parts that are particularly relevant to you. Some chapters have overlapping themes that apply to multiple nuances of similar fears. Some chapters completely contradict one another because different people fear different things and fears are all too often paradoxical even in the same person—which is quite scary!

Pay attention to the fact that the publishing section is the longest. This is the part of the writing job that takes us away from the safety of our desks, out of the warm little caves of our imaginations, and into the bright, cold world where others' judgments are waiting for us. We're social animals. We depend on attachment and belonging to survive, so it makes sense that we have so much fear about what powers other people could hold over us when we put our words into the world.

It's time to lay those fears to rest.

DISCLAIMER

I am not a psychologist, psychiatrist, counselor, doctor or health care professional of any kind. I am a writer who has dealt with and still deals with a lot of fear and anxiety in many areas of life.

This book is not intended as health care and should never replace professional advice.

This book has been written out of what I've learned and am continuing to learn in my journey. The ideas here are offered in the hope that my thoughts, experiences, and insights might inspire you in your journey.

If you are struggling with mental health issues related to fear, anxiety, or anything else, please reach out to an appropriate professional.

WHAT IS FEAR?

It's okay to have fear. It's normal and helpful to be afraid. Fear is our nervous system's way of protecting us, keeping us safe and warm in our cozy spaces so we can survive the harsh world and live to see another day. Yet our world has evolved, while our brains haven't. The same fear systems within us that protected us from cave bears (are cave bears a thing?) still send us into high danger alert about the correct placement of commas, about making up a fictional tale, about having an idea about the world and wanting to share it with others, about someone out there not liking what we have to say. That's why these fears about writing and publishing are so confusing. Writing is not actually life-threatening! Yet we still sit at our writing desks, poised to run, too paralyzed to act, confused about whether we should do either.

I'm not suggesting that we throw out all the publishing guidelines and ignore all the stylistic conventions, but I am suggesting, stating, and even pleading that we all go a little easier on ourselves when it comes to the fears of a writer. I'm suggesting that we all see the fears for what they are. Fears. Thoughts. Worries. And they can all be erased, changed, or rendered insignificant with new strategies and the mindset shifts I offer in this book.

Fear is an emotion, one of our core feelings, hardwired deep in our primal brains.

Fear is not bad. It serves a protective purpose in steering us away from danger. We can never eradicate fear, nor should we want to. In many of the chapters in this book I suggest ways to rethink situations, ways that we can inform our fear and demonstrate, with gratitude, that the emotion isn't necessary at that time. In other chapters there might not be a rethink, simply a situation where you have to pick your fear up, give it a hug, and carry it gently forward while you get on with your work.

WHO IS YOUR FEAR?

Many people recommend personifying fear. This is a decent exercise in separating one's self from fear as it demonstrates that we are beings with multiple parts, and fear is just one of them.

One writer I know thinks of her fear as an ugly little monster who sits around telling her not to do stuff. Her fear critter is well meaning but terribly stupid. Another writer I know pictures a host of little goblins, chattering at her from the sofa behind her writing desk. She turns her back and ignores them while she gets on with the work.

I tried this for a while, picturing my fear as a baby dragon (I named him Fafnir in homage to the Germanic dragon, who was mighty, but I always found his name a little silly). My Fafnir was cute, turquoise, and bumbling. He had a lot to complain about, but I always knew better. I talked to the dragon, tried to calm him down and get him to understand that he was scared only because he was little. But this didn't sit well with me. It was only a half truth.

In these examples, fear is pictured as something silly, small, ugly, harmless, something it's safe to ignore.

The more I went through my fear psychology (more on

that in the following section), the more the picture of my fear changed. So I made a new character out of my fear.

My fear isn't silly or insignificant, but my fear is still small, as in *young*. She's innocent.

My fear is my vulnerability.

My fear is a tall and powerful warrior. She's nameless. She stands in shining, elaborate plate armor, sword in hand, ready to fight, shield in hand, ready to protect. A poet at her heart, she's gentle and wise, but also she's fierce and brave and honorable, and she loves and serves me. She took on this role when we were both children, but I grew up a lot faster than she did. Sometimes she has trouble remembering that I'm an adult and I know a thing or two about the world, so I can see when she's not understanding a situation fully. She doesn't say much; she doesn't have to. Her presence is enough to feel, and it's up to me to apply the narrative. I can and often do change that narrative as I go along.

Of course I'm going to pay attention to a figure like that, and honor her role in my psyche. She's my protector but not my ruler, and she's welcome to come along on all my adventures. I'll listen honestly to her input, but ultimately, it's up to me to decide the ways we go.

HEARING ALL THE VOICES

We are all multitudinous beings.

There are other voices inside you besides fear—like the voices that brought you to the page in the first place.

Try listening to your imagination, your hope, love, strength, inspiration, and creative spirit. Try listening to these voices alongside your fear voice. Try listening to them first. Try trusting them.

Feel your fear, thank it for its service in attempting to protect you, and carry on writing with this other crowd of voices in the front seat with you.

MY PERSONAL STORY— HOW I CAME TO KNOW FEAR

What I've learned about fear psychology hasn't come directly through my writing life, or any formal study, but in the wake of dealing with a chronic neurological condition.

I was dizzy for about twelve years. Sometimes it was mild, sometimes it would disappear for brief periods. Sometimes it was like walking on rubber. Sometimes it was like the earth was dropping out from beneath my feet. Sometimes it was like someone was shaking my head violently from side to side. Sometimes it was gut churning vertigo that would turn the world upside down and have me on the floor. It was visual disturbances, it was tinnitus, it was brain fog so thick, some days I could barely recall my own name.

I had a million tests, and they all showed the same thing. There was nothing wrong with me. I tried dozens of medications and nothing worked. This kind of thing just sometimes happens, all the doctors said. They told me it was benign and to learn to live with it.

About ten years in, when I'd given up on ever getting a real answer or a cure, I discovered the world of mind-body work, specifically through the work of Dr. Yonit Arthur, The Steady Coach.

Mind-body syndromes are where the mind creates sensations in the body. It could be pain, or dizziness, or a host of other feelings. Doctors couldn't find anything wrong with me because there was nothing medically or physically wrong with me.

The dizziness is a nervous system dysregulation, a physical reaction to my fight-flight-freeze programming. My fears, and all kinds of other negative stress emotions I wasn't aware I had, were making me dizzy.

"You mean I can *think* my way out of this?" was my initial response on discovering this claim.

Not quite right. I had to *feel* my way out of it. And that's what I did.

Working with a therapist alongside Dr. Yo, and with so many amazing people in the mind-body community, I delved into fear psychology and looked my fear in the eye, looked myself in the soul. After more than a decade of suffering, at the time of writing this, I've been almost one hundred percent free of these chronic vertiginous sensations for over a year. When the sensations occasionally creep back in, there's always a reason, and that reason is always fear. I face the fear and everything clears.

What's this got to do with writing?

Facing my fears about writing and overcoming or managing them were a big part of my mind-body work. I'm not saying that my writing fears were at the core of all my anxiety, but they certainly played a starring role. I am a writer to my core. I've got ink in my veins, and my identity and self-worth and all kinds of values are tied up in my words. Of course my feelings about my writing were going to impact my overall nervous system.

I know fear. I might not have a psychological certification of any kind, but my personal journey with this thing and sharing that journey with other people going through similar conditions have given me a unique insight into my anxiety landscape, and common situations others also experience. In this book, I offer some of that insight to you, fellow writer.

You fear something about the writing life. If you didn't, you wouldn't have picked up this book. Whatever shape your fear comes in, you can get through it. You might conquer and eradicate the fear, you might not. But are you ready to look your fear in the eye, take it by the hand, and get on with becoming the writer you know you're meant to be?

Let's do this together.

If you have your own writing fears to manage, and ways to flip them, please share with me via email. My contacts are at the end of the book.

PART ONE
MINDSET

BEING MISUNDERSTOOD

What if people don't get me?

What if I'm misunderstood, my voice misconstrued, and my words totally miss the mark?

Will you let this fear stop you from writing, from attempting to get your voice heard in the first place?

Whether we're talking about the publishing world and public readers or people near and dear to our personal lives, there will be people who don't understand you. They might know you, like you, love you, and still just not get you.

It hurts to be misunderstood. It's frustrating and isolating. But a slight shift in mindset is all it takes to quell the fear of these hurts.

It's okay to be misunderstood.

Maybe it's a sign that your communication wasn't clear? Can you restate? Rephrase?

Maybe you're talking to the wrong people? Some people just can't understand, and that's okay too. Find the people who do get it.

Or simply rest knowing that differing opinions and views,

even disagreements, are valuable. It's what makes the world so interesting, and disagreement can be a point of learning on both sides.

You've got something to say. Your writing is a safe place for you to say it. Say it and see what happens.

SELF-DISCIPLINE

What if I don't have the self-discipline to be a writer?

I'll eventually fail at it, so why even start?

Yes, being a writer takes discipline. But so does showing up to any other job. The difference is that typically, writers require intrinsic discipline. We are our own professional accountability.

We need motivation to stay at the desk, motivation to keep coming back. Not everyone is cut out for the writing life. But many potential writers just don't know what self-discipline actually is or how to develop it, so they believe they're not cut out for it. They quit because that's the easier option.

So what is self-discipline?

Discipline is not the punitive punishments doled out to keep you in control.

Discipline is not forcing yourself down, chaining yourself to the desk when you really don't want to write.

Discipline has its roots in learning. Think "disciple."

We learn the value of a certain practice, and in seeking that value, we find the motivation to stay on that path.

What's the value of you writing? Of you coming back to

the page, day after day? Does leaving the desk, not writing, have a greater value to you? Then that's the path you'll be drawn to.

Discipline is learning what you want to *be* as much as what you want to *do*. In learning to *be* that state, you simply *do* the thing. That's how writers create self-discipline. We practice it.

LOSING THE PASSION

There are many reasons a writer might need or want to slow down on writing.

Maybe it's a time constraint. Maybe it's an energy problem. Whatever it is, when we put our writing life on the chopping block, it might make us wonder if our passion for writing is at risk. This can be scary.

Does needing to slow down mean we've already lost the passion?

Does this mean we will lose the passion?

Will the writing wait for us?

Many writers who feel this way are writers to their core. Writing is not only something we do, but it feels like something that we are.

If writing can't be your focus right now, you need not panic.

You will not lose writing. You will not lose your passion or drive as much as you will not lose your breath when you slow down to rest. Writing is part of your life.

If that needs to change in some way, that's okay. It's temporary. Writing will come back.

The passion for writing may fade for other reasons. Maybe

it's just not your thing anymore. This might bring up all manner of guilt, shame, and fear.

Does this mean I'm a failure?

Does this mean I'm a quitter?

Quite the opposite.
We change. We grow. It's part of being a fulfilled human.
If writing was once something you loved and it no longer is, then that's okay. You've changed. Welcome that. You're allowed to change.
Embrace whatever new passions come in to fill that space, secure in the knowledge that you have explored a part of yourself through writing, that you have tried, and lived, and moved on.
Let your passion for writing burn like a romance. It can blaze, or it can simmer. It can be brief and intense, or it can be a stable, eternal warmth. Either way, it's life-changing.

FAILURE

There are so many ways a writer might feel they have failed.

Poor sales, bad reviews, no subscribers, no followers, agent rejection, publisher rejection.

Struggling to write a book. Being unable to write a book. Missing a writing session. Missing a month of writing sessions. It goes on.

The first list is external.

Those things are totally out of a writer's control. We can influence them in various ways, but there's nothing we can do about any of it. We can tweak tactics, encourage sales, entice followers, but that only goes so far.

There's no failure here. We can only fail at what we do. We can only fail with actions that are in our control.

A critical review isn't a failure. It's a reader who didn't like your book. It happens to every single book ever written.

Poor sales isn't a failure. The publishing market is such a chaotic and fickle universe that not even the top publishers fully understand why books sell (ever wondered why Random House is called Random House?). Poor sales on otherwise good books is just a crapshoot.

As for the second list, these are things that are in our control; they are internal.

We will fail to write a book if we do not sit down to write a book.

What's the real, deep fear in the face of this prospect?

If I fail to write this book, I will be disappointed in myself.

Why?

Because I wanted to write the book and I didn't.

Why is that scary?

Because it means I'm not what I thought I could be.

It means I'm not as valuable as I thought I could be.

Why didn't you write the book?

Because I'm scared to fail.

Your value, your potential, your worth have nothing to do with whether or not you wrote a book. You have value and worth because you simply exist, and you can never fail at that.

Write the book and you won't fail at writing a book.

If you don't write the book, then you won't fail at learning something about yourself and growing as a result.

Failure is a mindset. With little shifts, we can change the entire concept of failure.

Failure always has an upside. It leads us to different paths. It teaches us things about ourselves. A successful person in any field stands upon a great mountain of past failures and looks toward a bright future of many more.

If you fear making a mistake, then don't get out of bed. Which in itself is a mistake, because who wants to live like that? Mistakes are how we learn. Mistakes are how we realize what we want, what works, and what to do next.

Aim to fail!

Failure is only a defeat if you choose for it to be.

HUMILIATION

When you're a publishing writer, it's likely you're going to screw up somehow and experience humiliation.

You might publish something with factual inaccuracies, typos, a crappy cover your inexperienced eyes led you to believe was great. You might make a gaffe on social media in the heat of the moment. The ways an author might feel humiliated are many.

Humiliation is painful.

But these types of humiliations, while they might sting in the short term, aren't anything to fear.

If you've published something wrong, pull it down and republish it (indie luxury!). If you say something online that you shouldn't have, swallow your pride and apologize. If you're in a situation where you can't unpublish, just wait. The world will forget, even if you don't.

You might feel humiliated that your book doesn't sell well, or that no one comes to a book launch event. Is any of this stuff in your control? Did you do everything you could to make it work?

Like so much emotional work, if we look into the definitions of the feelings, we can find ways to calm them.

Humiliation is a type of shame, and the distinction

between humiliation and similar feelings is important here. You feel humiliated when someone criticizes you for something and we don't feel we deserve that sense of unworthiness. No one deserves to feel like a bad person if they publish a typo or write something untrue. It simply does not matter.

The serious problems here come when you feel true shame or guilt for these mistakes. You feel like you've done a terrible thing (that's guilt), or you might feel you yourself are terrible because of it (that's shame). No one deserves these feelings over a publishing error.

When you realize every writer makes these minor mistakes, then humiliation, guilt or shame can turn into embarrassment. It smarts, but it's fleeting, maybe even funny, and we all move on. No lasting harm done and nothing to fear.

You're not a bad person for making mistakes. You're simply a person.

SOMEONE FINDING OUT

Argh! What if I put myself out there, publish my books, and start making writer friends, and they find out?!

Find out what?

That I'm not a brilliant writer? That I don't know everything about writing? That I don't know everything about writing even in my genre? That I'm making it up as I go along? That I....

You're not expected to be The Best or have all the answers. And guess what? The person you're worried about failing in this sense is also having these same worries.

No one knows all the things. Every writer is still learning, even those with ten books or more published. The publishing world is constantly changing and we're all always learning.

These feelings are a symptom of impostor syndrome, and as we'll soon see, that's nothing to fear either.

IMPOSTOR SYNDROME

Impostor syndrome is weird.

It's a feeling that you don't belong within a certain sphere of the writing community, that you're not good enough. That you're a fraud, and that someone will call you out on it. See previous chapter on Someone Finding Out.

Two things define impostor syndrome: One, that icky feeling that you're not enough or don't belong because of a lack of skills or credentials. Two, evidence to the contrary.

Why would you be in the writing community if you weren't a writer, if you weren't good enough? If you didn't know enough about writing, you wouldn't have written a book.

If someone thinks you're fraudulent, and you're not, isn't that a problem for them, not you?

True impostors don't actually have impostor syndrome. They might experience guilt or shame about their fraudulence, but it's not the same thing. Impostor syndrome is only felt by people who do belong where they fear they don't.

Writers can also fear impostor syndrome in itself. This is a state of not only having the fears that make up impostor syndrome (I'm not worthy!), but also suffering the effect of those fears.

Very much like other fears relating to writing, impostor syndrome is a good sign that you're pushing yourself, widening your boundaries, and learning, ever upward. If you ever start to relax, thinking, "Yep, I'm the best, so I'm done learning," then it's really time to worry.

CALLING YOURSELF A WRITER

The label "writer" has so much social pressure that some writers are afraid to even apply it to themselves.

Why is that?

Because we fear we're not living like Hemingway, or writing like Margaret Atwood, or publishing like Stephen King. We fear we're not writer enough to earn the title.

Many writers tack on "aspiring" as a prefix. But this is just as damaging as it places that writer in a passive null state.

If you're writing, then you're a writer. Maybe you're aspiring to be a "published writer," but that's different.

If you write, label yourself a writer. Own it.

Only one person in the world can and will write like Margaret Atwood, and she's already doing it. Only one person in the world can publish like Stephen King and he's doing it. And as for Hemingway, do you really want to emulate his lifestyle?

Only one person in the world can be a writer like you.

You write. You're a writer. Even if it's not the way you earn your money. You're a writer.

BEING OVERSHADOWED

The world is full of books and writers. How does a writer or a book stand out? It's a daunting prospect, particularly when the promotional strategies we need to overcome this invisibility in themselves can be scary.

Consider this mindset shift. You are unlikely to ever stand out in the world of books as a whole. Few authors do, and even those at the top of the lists won't be on every reader's mind.

So, shrink the world.

You don't need to stand out to the world, just a few people. Even just one to start with.

You're writing for a practically microscopic sliver of the entire book industry. Just because there are giants standing above you doesn't mean you cannot thrive in the undergrowth. If this still doesn't quell your fear, remember also that those giant authors grew from small beginnings.

IRRELEVANCE

We all want our lives to mean something, our writing to make some manner of meaningful impact.

What happens if it doesn't?

What happens if we're irrelevant or forgotten?

It's a hard truth to consider, but most people seem irrelevant if we look at the universe as a whole. Our lives, our books, feel like insignificant blips in existence.

Nihilism never did anyone any good, and I personally believe that we're all valuable, even as nanoscopic blips in an infinite universe. But that might too big a scale to think about. So, consider a smaller universe.

Start with yourself.

Your writing, your entire life, needs only to have relevance for one person.

You.

Even if we shift the conversation out of existential ideas of meaning and think of only cultural meaning, our world is such a tangle of infinite, ever-changing cultures that no one thing will have relevance to all or even most.

So to worry about your writing being irrelevant is to worry about not noticing a single seed in the Amazon jungle.

Just like that jungle, our world is made up of the many.

Many places, many life forms. Each tiny part contributes to the stunning and magical biodiversity that makes the entire system thrive.

So thrive in your own little part of the universe, see your own relevance and decide what that means to the entire jungle, and even if it needs to mean anything.

You will change the world with your writing by being one person who is fulfilling their desires, who is creating and cultivating meaning instead of mindless consumption of junk. Imagine if more people in the world did that. Make that your meaning. Make your own relevance to your own world.

EXISTENTIAL USELESSNESS

I am just a writer.
I don't save lives.
I don't invent technology that will heal the earth, or explore new planets to inhabit after we've ruined this one.
I'm not a world-changing thought leader.
I can't build a house for a family to live in, or farm food for a family to eat.
I make up stories. Fake ones.
What use am I?
Am I even needed in society?

A lot of these voices called out during the pandemic, as many a writer turned away from the page to focus on other things. But it's not just the pandemic that had writers questioning the wider social importance of their work. Writers, and all artists, have wondered this and feared their irrelevance since the Industrial Revolution and the birth of capitalism.

The earliest humans told stories and recorded them.

Storytelling is our birthright.

Artists and storytellers once had a secure place in society as bards, clerics, holy figures, mystics, philosophers, minstrels, and the like.

Along the way, we held on to these roles, but we locked them away with exalted preciousness that they were otherworldly, far away from the common. The makers of more worldly things, the people who made the money and set the laws, became the visible ones.

In this industrialized capitalist world, it's all too easy to feel the messaging that our work isn't important. It doesn't get done in the massive glass skyscrapers that define our cities, it doesn't build anything to live in, it doesn't grow food, it doesn't cure our bodies when they suffer.

But you know why writers and all artists are critical to the world; otherwise you wouldn't be following this vocation. You might need a little reminding, though…

Artists create meaning. It's the writers we turn to when we want truths expressed, feelings solidified, the universe understood not in terms of atoms but in terms of what it actually means. That's why we have poet laureates, government-sponsored grants, and the rest of it. That's why the figures of the artist became exalted and out of reach.

We artists serve as examples to the rest. Imagine how the world might look where all people were allowed to follow their passions, to work in vocations that suited their souls, not just what was available at the time or what was decided would earn the most money. Work that provided solace and support and understanding to hearts and minds and bodies everywhere. Our world is more messed up than ever. Every generation claims they're living in the darkest days, but doesn't it feel more true right here and now? The only way out is through passion and connection and understanding and real authentic living (not hashtag authenticity).

We writers must take this responsibility very seriously. The fate of the world depends on us.

AUTHORITY

Who am I to write this book?

Often writers worry about not having the appropriate authority to tell the story they want to tell.

That authority might come as a formal credential, or it might come as a less-formal life experience.

This cannot be explained away with a simple mindset shift, for every type of writer writing every type of book. Some books, particularly in the nonfiction space, need to be written by certain definable authorities. But for other kinds of books, authority is not so easily defined.

The words "author" and "authority" share the same roots. In the act of writing, of authoring, you are putting your name to some form of statement. You, author, get to decide what that statement is and what right you have to put your name to it. If you believe in that but others in the world don't, then settle it as a difference of opinion.

If that still isn't enough, there are ways to increase your authority. Get help. Work with others and borrow their authority. Gain a credential. Research and ensure you're writing on solid ground.

THE UNKNOWN

The question "What if…?" appears frequently in this book. If anxiety could be summed up in a single phrase, "What if…?" fits perfectly.

"What if…?" is the articulation of the fear of the unknowable future.

What if my book doesn't sell?

What if I get a scathing review?

What if I'm not good enough?

What if I never reach the success I dream of?

I'm not sure there's a way to ever get rid of the "What if…?" panic if that's the way your brain is wired.

It's one of those annoying moments when fear is just there, and we have to sit alongside it, take its hand, and keep on working and living. But there are ways to make this fear of the unknown smaller, more manageable, and lighter to carry.

Next time you're struck by "What if…?", answer the question.

What if you never reach your career goals? What might that mean? What might that look like? What might you do instead? Will you be okay?

At the end of many "What if...?" questions, we will find an answer that might look different from our ideal outcome. We might never write a book. We might never make a living from our writing. But in most cases in writing and publishing, we will eventually be okay whatever happens.

If everything is likely to turn out okay, in whatever shape that takes, then there's really nothing to fear.

FEAR

"We have nothing to fear but fear itself," said Franklin Delano Roosevelt.

Nope. We don't even need to fear that.

Being afraid of any aspect of the writer's life or craft doesn't mean you're doing it wrong, or that you're timid or unworthy.

It means that you're in a new place, exploring unchartered territory, out of your comfort zone. It means you're learning, pushing yourself to new heights, growing.

This is a good thing.

Feel the fear. Make it your ally and use it to grow.

PART TWO
CREATIVITY

UNORIGINALITY

My ideas are unoriginal.

I'm a reductive hack.

I have nothing new to offer the world.

These are fears many of us have had.

If you're a new writer, chances are you will write fairly stock-standard stuff. This is a good thing, and nothing to fear.

Every musician starts out playing scales and covers. Every painter starts out copying the techniques of those who have painted before.

Derivation is how we learn.

When the musician's fingers are getting used to walking those scales and shaping those chords, they will start to embellish with their own arrangements; the painters will start to flourish in new colors and shapes. The tropes and stories you imitate will twist and morph into new and exciting ideas.

Original thinking stems from what has come before. Combine existing ideas and repurpose them through the lens of your own experience—that is the very essence of creative thinking. Follow that, and there's no way you can be unoriginal.

WRITING SOMETHING PERSONAL

What if someone sees me?

Writing yourself onto the page is an exposure. Even if you're writing the most fanciful fiction, parts of you are in those words, those characters, and their stories.

Sometimes that's deep and raw and renders us vulnerable to the world. While it can be wonderfully therapeutic to write yourself out like this, it's also terrifying.

What if someone reads it?

Even worse, what if someone reads it and judges it harshly? Judges *you* harshly?

Yes, this is scary stuff, and one of those fears we just learn to carry gently.

There are two general approaches to managing this fear of getting really personal.

The first approach, which might be a lot easier for some, is to write it in secret. Pen names are incredibly common and many writers choose to write with complete anonymity under a pseudonym. Secret identities are cool! Run with it and spill yourself into your words without fear.

The second approach is to feel the fear and do it anyway.

If you're writing yourself so openly onto your page, then you're likely looking to create something authentic, something with purpose, something that will connect in someone else. In writing, or anywhere else in life, we get to that connection by being vulnerable, by exposing those raw nerves. Someone might read those words and offer you sympathy, empathy, awe, gratitude and all the good things that happen when we really connect with other humans. Or someone might read them and react with vitriol. You can't control either reaction.

Whether someone loves or hates your writing, it's nothing to do with you. People bring themselves to their judgments, good or bad, and a reader will make your words what they need them to be. Your *words*, not *you*. I know it's hard to differentiate when we write personal stuff, but it's important to practice.

Your role is in the writing, not the receiving, so write that role with your all. When the reactions come, good or bad, welcome them. You've made a connection from your truest self.

CREATIVE STAGNATION

Day in, day out, book after book, you're writing the same thing. It can get stale. It can stop the words from flowing altogether.

Many writers fear this state of creative stagnation when they're in it. Many new writers fear this becoming a state, so resist starting.

Creative stagnation is dull and lifeless.

Creative stagnation is boredom.

But boredom isn't death. Boredom is a valuable privilege.

If you're bored, you have everything you need—you have the basic necessities settled.

When we get bored, our minds automatically look for something to alleviate the discomfort. That's an exercise in creative thinking. We get drawn out of boredom to the things that naturally appeal to us. Topics to explore, processes to experiment with. If you listen closely, boredom can direct you to new ideas, new activities that are authentically you.

So do not fear this stagnant period. Wallow in the boredom, use it. Listen to it and notice how, without even trying, you will lead yourself to inspiration.

PIGEONHOLING

When we look at the market of successful authors, we typically see that the authors doing the best in sales, backlist size, reviews, and all those external metrics are the authors who are focused on one genre.

Focus can bring success, but for some, this focus can also bring a fear that they are pigeonholed and stuck in that hole. The world has an expectation of them, and to break that expectation is to threaten their success.

Many new and emerging writers fear this threat before they've even established themselves into a hole in the first place.

This is a fear protecting our creative spirit, and it comes from a perception of an external threat. A threat that may or may not exist.

Here's the solution to that fear…

Write whatever you want.

If you're established in one genre and want to write something different, you're allowed to do that. Readers aren't dumb. They will see that this new creative adventure differs from what they know you for. Some will come along for the ride, others won't. It doesn't matter. This is your adventure.

Or, if you really are too fearful of the threat of this disruption to your brand, then write this new thing with a new name. Tell no one. Let this truly be just for you.

If you're a would-be writer carrying this fear and it's stopping you from starting, please just start.

Being pigeonholed into a genre you're too established to break from easily is a luxurious problem to have. Write your stories and then see if it's a problem that needs fearing. Chances are it's just a projected anxiety from some other place that your fear has conjured up to stop you from writing and publishing.

OTHER FORMS OF ART

You are a writer.

This doesn't mean that you can't dabble in or even become known for other forms of artistic expression.

Try anything and everything.

Painting, sketching, music, film, textiles, pottery, dance. Make all the things.

If you fear that this will take precious time away from your writing, then remember creative divergence.

Creative divergence is the process of dabbling in one method of creative exploration in order to expand other areas. So in effect, taking time off your writing to playfully explore other art forms will enhance your writing.

Writers need experiences to draw from. New forms of art can be that experience as much as anything else. You're allowed to be more than one thing. You're allowed to do more than one thing. You're allowed to do all the things.

RUNNING OUT OF IDEAS

When you first came to the page as a writer, you had an idea.

You might just have one idea at the beginning, and for some, this is terrifying.

You want to be a writer, but how is that possible if you only have one idea?

What happens when I use it up?

What if I run out of ideas?

What if I only have enough ideas for one book?

This. Will. Not. Happen.

Writers naturally have ideas. Remember, it was your idea that sat you down at the keyboard in the first place. Unless you simply had a burning desire to just sit in a room alone typing, and if so, there are other, far easier (and potentially more lucrative) careers that will fulfill that need for you.

Sure, we can feel like our ideas stagnate or dry up, or aren't as plentiful as we'd like them to be. But that's not a symptom of having *no* ideas. It just means your creative fuel tank is low.

When the creative tank is dry, it can feel like you'll never have another idea in your life, or all your current ideas stink.

But tanks are for refilling.

Explore the world. Be curious. Read, watch, listen. Consume and participate in the world, and do it in weird ways. Actively seek ideas, write, and more ideas will come—and I promise the fear of no ideas will dissolve in the wake of more ideas than you know what to do with. And that might bring another fear...

HAVING TOO MANY IDEAS

I have more ideas for books than I have life left to write all those books. I'm not alone in this.

That's a mildly depressing prospect if thought about from a certain angle, and for some it's a truth laden in fear.

Having too many ideas can create a sense of time scarcity, an anxiety that we'll be left unfinished. We rush to get it all out, but more ideas just keep on coming. That's what writing does.

Just write.

We give our time to the ideas that are important, and sometimes it's not up to us to decide what's important.

Shift your mindset. An overflow of ideas is a full tank, and that means you have all the creative fuel you need to write the books you do have time to write.

PART THREE
CRAFT

CLICHÉS

Urgh. This is so cliché.

Cliché is a writer's state of terror. To be accused of cliché is to have been told you're no good, you're boring, you're not valuable.

Yes, clichés are unoriginal, but that doesn't mean they can't be used in some way, made fresh, turned around, or proven wrong.

Don't avoid writing something because you fear it's a cliché. Write it. If it doesn't work out, tweak it, edit it, play with it and see what happens. Experiment with clichés as ingredients in a new and fantastic recipe that only you have the power to concoct.

Clichés didn't start as maligned, overused tropes. They became that way because whatever they contain resonated so deeply with audiences that people just kept on using them and using them. Unfortunately, like anything in life, too much of a good thing lessens its worth.

You have the power to use that original resonance, find that core value, and breathe a new life into it. Embrace the cliché! Make it your own.

SHORT STORIES

Short stories are tricky, condensed forms with complexity beyond their length. Short stories are hard to write and even harder to sell, so it's no wonder so many writers fear them and so many avoid them.

But some writers want to write short stories and still hold this fear.

So how do we overcome this fear?

Write short stories.

Find the readers that love short stories.

Write more short stories.

YOU'RE NOT SKILLED ENOUGH FOR YOUR IDEAS

Many a writer faces the page with an idea so fabulous that it defies belief. That writer then starts to write, and the words just can't do justice to that initial concept. The ideas flounder. The spark goes out. The writer gives up.

It's a scary prospect.

What if I'm never good enough to write my ideas?

Every idea becomes something different once it hits the page. It's part of the creative process.

Instead of lamenting that your writing is not of the same quality as your idea, sit back and marvel at the entirely new and unexpected thing you have made. Set out on the journey with your fledgling idea and wait with patience and curiosity and excitement to see what it will turn out to be.

An idea is nothing—it's a pattern of impulses in a network of neurons. A story, a book, that's a real thing, something born out of an idea that grows into life. Aren't you excited to see what your idea grows up to be?

Yet a writer typing away, waiting to see what their idea becomes, still might not have the skills to do what they feel is justice to this vision.

It's a common situation, and there are typically two options to address this fear.

One: Write other things first. Study and write and improve your skills, then go back to your magnum opus.

Two: Write it all now. Feel the fear and do it anyway. Respect the fear as a sign that this project means something to you. Pour it all in as best you can and work at it until it feels right to you (or close enough to right, which is the reality that most writers face). Don't hold back.

Would you rather hone your craft on works of your heart or practice pieces waiting for a time when you feel ready—a time that may or may not come?

DEFINING YOUR OWN BOOK LENGTHS

Traditionally published books are as long as they are because that's what worked in the beginning of the book trade. Shelves in stores determined the "best" length for books because of spine width and what was most easily visible. Most commercial novels are at least an inch thick because spines on anything smaller are harder to read.

In the twenty-first century, book length is now irrelevant. The market still sits with certain lengths of books, but plenty of authors are defining their own sweet spot when it comes to the kinds of stories that work best for them and doing just fine. Yes, even short epic fantasy is now a thing.

Write your story and let it be as long or as short as it needs to be.

DEFINING YOUR OWN CHAPTER LENGTHS

Is this too short to be a chapter?

Is this chapter too long?

How long should a chapter be, anyway?

How long is a piece of string? How long should a piece of string be?

As long as it needs to be in order to be of use.

This fear is based on the false belief that you need permission to write in a certain way. If you feel you need permission to write super-short or super-long chapters, or mix both in the same book, then grant yourself that permission.

Your actions will be the permission slip for the next writer.

BAD PROSE

What if my writing is terrible?

Every writer will write crappy prose at some point in their careers. Some of it is even published. Some of it is wildly successful. Like seriously, some unbelievably terrible writing has become unbelievably successful. One person's "bad" prose is another person's favorite novel.

What is bad prose anyway?

Prose that breaks grammar rules? Every book in the world (except maybe *The Elements of Style*) does this to some degree.

Prose that breaks current stylistic conventions? That's how new styles, genres, and markets are born.

The only way to really write bad prose is to write in a way that confuses the reader, a way that doesn't clearly communicate the story and its world into the reader's head.

Write. Keep writing and polishing your words, learning the craft, and reading the words that *you* decide make good writing. That's how not to write bad prose.

WORD COUNTS

It's so many words!

I'll never get that done!

What if I don't have what it takes to write that much?

Whether it's a daily word count or the overall length of a piece, fearing a word count is just fearing the work.
    Most (all?) writers love writing, so what's to fear? Epic novels of hundreds of thousands of words are written in the same way as one hundred word short stories: one word after the other.
    You can write one word, can't you?

WRITING WITH MULTIPLE POINTS OF VIEW

This issue has come up in every single writers' group I have ever been a part of, and it's usually asked in fear, like risking one way over the other is a death sentence.

Should I write with single or multiple points of view?

The answers vary.

Commonly, writers are told it depends on the genre and story. This is true to a point.

But there is a dominance of advice telling newer authors to stick with a single POV.

Why?

Because it's easier to keep track of. Does that mean a new writer shouldn't write multiple POVs?

Sure, writing in multiple POVs can be tricky, but it's certainly not impossible.

Even if your genre is widely single POV, it doesn't mean your story has to be.

How does your story want to be written?

Tell your fear to stand down.

It doesn't matter if you write it one way and have to change it midway through the manuscript. It doesn't matter if you write it as a complete and published book and then have reviewers tell you they hated the POV split. You can try something new in your next book. It's also possible that the multiple POV will be a raging success, adding depth and vibrancy to a brilliant story.

There's only one way to tell which way it will go for you and your story, and that way will not end in death and torture, just words on a page.

DIVERSITY

Not every character you write will be or should be a representation of you and your immediate life.

The real world is full of wildly different people living wildly different lives in wildly different cultures. That's diversity. It's a beautiful thing.

So why should the world in our books be different?

Many authors fear writing about what's different from them. Often, this fear comes from a good place. We fear getting a representation of a person not like ourselves wrong. We fear being insensitive, or naive, or simply accidentally ignorant. And that's a good fear to have.

If you're attempting to write diverse characters, and you're worried about getting your representation wrong, this fear is the exact motivation you need to get it right.

Research. Observe. Ask people. Employ a sensitivity reader to ensure you've got your representations accurate and fair.

WRITING IN A NEW GENRE

Our fears like to keep us in the familiar territory where we know the rules and the landscape. Fear keeps us in safe places. Genre is one such place.

Many a writer will stand at the edge of a new genre, curious but too scared to step in. It's a fear of getting it wrong, of not liking the new terrain, of getting lost in the new terrain, of what others in that world might say about your adventures.

But it's okay, it's safe. If a genre exists and you have a yen to go there, then go there. If the genre doesn't exist and you have a yen to go there, then make it exist by going there.

Try it and see what happens. Study this new and exciting place and the others who formed it before you. Read the classics and the new releases, or forge a fresh path. If your story ends up working but you're still not sure of this new territory, you can always publish with a pen name, and if it doesn't go well, move on to the next thing.

Many a writer will feel an urge to play in other genres; then they write a first draft, and the urge vanishes. They return home at least knowing what was outside the borders. Others find a new home. It's okay to have more than one home.

ELEGANT PROSE

The fear of not being able to write elegant prose is related to the fear of writing bad prose, but more specifically, this is a fear of not being able to write this particular stye of prose.

Elegant prose is the style we tend to see in literary fiction. It's rich in symbolism and metaphor, uses big words and lots of technicalities. It's poetic and lyrical. Somewhere along the way, Western culture decided this defined "good" writing. Ergo, writers who don't write in this style are "bad" writers.

This simply isn't true.

Good writing is clear and engaging storytelling, and that comes in many stylistic forms, even those yet to be established. Many writers will ruin a perfectly good story by trying so hard to push their style into elegant prose that the words are overwritten, flowery, convoluted. By trying to write well, they write badly. We call this Purple Prose. Which is a shame, because purple is my favorite color.

Elegant prose is just a style. It's no more valuable than any other style and doesn't need to have this cultural exaltation applied to it. It's not something to strive for as much as it isn't something to be avoided. If it's your way, then embrace that and write. If it's not, then embrace whatever is your style and write without fear that what you're doing is lesser or wrong.

NOT WRITING AS WELL AS WE USED TO

In the writing world, we all tend to agree that writers get better over time. It makes sense that we would, right?

But it's a truth that some authors have incredibly good work, perhaps even their best work, already behind them.

This is a scary prospect.

It connects to the fear that we will never advance our skills, but in this sense, a skill declines. The results of our best efforts in anything can and will change over time, but this might not be a linear upward path. Our next book might not be as good as the one before it.

Who's to say this will happen to you? It's an unknowable future, a literal anxiety.

So, what's the best way to handle any anxious thoughts? Look at the here and now.

A writer near the beginning of their journey writes in the best way they can now. If, in five years, that book doesn't read so well, then that's a problem for a time that doesn't exist. Does it mean this writer hasn't done their best? No.

Do your best now. That's all that matters and nothing to fear.

Your best today will be different from your best tomorrow. Not necessarily better, nor worse, just different.

PART FOUR
PROCESS

AI TECHNOLOGY

At this time of my writing this (early 2024), generative AI is one of the biggest fears in the writing community.

It's polarizing. AI is exciting for some authors as we look toward all the creative possibilities this new toy enables. For others, AI is terrifying as we lament the rise of the robot writer and the death of the author. The reality lies, as it so often does, in the middle.

The writing bots are not going away. Just like this internet thing is not going away. Generative AI is not only not going back in the box, it is going to advance. It will become more capable and it will become ubiquitous.

There is nothing to fear here.

Yes, there are concerns. There are intellectual property dilemmas. Some people will use generative AI to cheat and manipulate. Most won't. This makes it the same as any other tool humans have invented or discovered, just like the rest of the internet.

Does the fact that the internet is an ethical minefield, that it harbors all the worst humanity has to offer, stop you from harnessing its power for good, or at the very least accepting its existence with neutrality? Because that's where we will end up with generative AI.

AI-written books are a thing and they will become even more of a thing as the technology develops.

The world will learn to cope, just as we learned to cope with the advent of photography and the printing press, technology that was deeply mistrusted at its advent as well. Photography and printing have not brought about the death of the artist and generative AI will not bring about the death of the writer.

Generative AI enables the development of different kinds of writers, of AI writers, of AI-assisted writers, and there will still be room for writers who choose to write without AI at all. You get to decide where you and your art sits, and do so without fearing other authors who are making different decisions.

Get to know the technology and you'll get to know your fears around it. Get to know your fears and you'll be able to quiet them.

AN UNFOCUSED WRITING CAREER

Writers love productivity advice, and one piece of advice we hear a lot is to focus on one thing.

Write one project at a time.

Write in one genre.

Focus on one niche.

For some writers, this is golden advice. It eliminates distractions, enables a deep exploration of one area, and promotes high productivity.

For other writers, it's a creativity killer and a shackle on their minds, souls and process. Some writers just can't help themselves, jumping from project to project.

These multi-minded writers can come to fear their apparent lack of focus as an obstacle to their success.

It's not.

There is no need to fear a lack of focus.

Yes, you are allowed to write in as many fields as you want.

Embrace it as a creative superpower and as an expression of your rich and varied mind.

Sure, when it comes to getting the words done, it typically pays to single task on a project, at least for each writing session, but that doesn't mean that writers with a multi-passionate, unfocused creative agenda cannot have a highly productive and fulfilling writing life.

BALANCING MULTIPLE WRITING PROJECTS

Multi-minded writers who embrace a multi-passionate life and want to write all the things require an element of balance.

This balancing act can be a fearful prospect.

What if nothing ever gets completed?

What if the writing doesn't delve as deep as it could?

What if I get confused and overwhelmed and I burn out?

Writing multiple projects at once can be tricky, but it's not at all impossible, and it's a fruitful and satisfying way to write for many.

Just try it.

Devise your own scales.

A little of this project in the morning, and that one in the afternoon. A first draft of this followed by a revision draft of that. Ideation on fiction one day, drafting nonfiction the next. There are so many options. It will take some experimenting, but if writing on multiple projects is something that you want to do, a process that suits your cognitive styles, then you will make it happen in a cohesive way.

FAILING A PROCESS

What if I try this and it doesn't work?

That writer swears by morning writing, but what if it makes me too tired?

Writing at night is the only time I have, but what if I can't focus when I'm up that late?

I read about fast drafting, but what if it's too messy and I get overwhelmed?

Outlining a book seems like a good idea, but what if it's too boring and I lose interest?

What if I try it this or that way and I fail?

There are as many ways to be a writer as there are writers, and every single person who has ever written a book has their own process for doing so. And every single one of those processes was developed by trying it one way first. Some writers nail it the first time. Most don't.

Try on a process and see what fits. If it doesn't work, then what have you lost? Nothing. You still got some writing done, right?

If that process doesn't work, you have gained the knowledge that it's not your process, and you can move on with confidence.

When you find a method that fits you well, wear that process in until it feels like your second skin, and if it ever wears out or you change and it no longer fits, try a new one and evolve.

INABILITY TO FINISH A PROJECT

What if I don't have what it takes to finish this book?

Writing the start of a book or story is very different from writing the end, and writing that middle might be the most difficult part of all. What if you can't get through that middle and never reach the end?

You can get through it. Writing session by writing session, word by word. The middle will form and the ending will appear.

But what if it doesn't?

Or, more accurately, what if you don't *want* to finish?

What if the story is in such a mess that it's too hard to fix? Or it's simply taking too much to write, and it's all too hard?

First, figure out what's really the fear here.

Is it that you fear that finishing this book is out of your skill range?

Or is it that it's too much, or not worthy of your energy to complete?

If it's the first and you *want* to finish it, then write it as best you can. Improving a poorly written draft is exactly what revision is for. And we all write bad books in the first draft.

If you don't actually *want* to finish this book, then don't.

It's simple and safe to quit, and sunk-cost fallacy is a thing even writers need to consider.

But I advise quitting with a caveat.

Writers need to learn how to write to the end of books for the reasons I opened this chapter with. Endings are different, middles are different, openings are different. If you only ever start projects, you become excellent at openings and completely incapable of middles and ends because you've never gotten there.

So if the book is simply not what you want, do consider writing to the end just to learn how to do it, and then shove it in a drawer, never to be thought of again.

Nothing terrible will happen to you if you abandon a work in progress. It's your creative life. But you might not feel so great if you continually abandon projects and never make headway on your overall writing goals. So just be clear on what flavor of fear is keeping you from reaching the end.

INABILITY TO FINISH A SERIES

If there's one thing harder than writing one book, it's writing three books all linked together. Or six, or nine, or hundreds.

Writing a series is a slog, and many writers, after writing that first book or first few books, fear they won't have what it takes to complete the series.

But you can get there. Not all at once, and likely not quickly, but

book by book.

You wrote one book, you can write another. One word at a time, one book at a time.

Remember, once you establish that series world, things get a little easier. The setting, characters, and major plots are already in place, so that's some of the heavy lifting already taken care of.

Of course, it can get boring writing in the same world. So if that's the source of your fear of not getting through a series, take some time to creatively refresh. Consider what enticed you about this world to start writing that first book. Write something different, or take a break from writing altogether.

PROCRASTINATION

Procrastination is a nasty word. It's the opposite of the world's golden ideals of productivity, of advancement, and worth. Procrastination is lazy and useless, and anyone who finds themselves procrastinating ought to feel ashamed of themselves and their dirty, lazy habits. Well, that's what it feels like we're being told when we read anything about how procrastination needs to be avoided like a disease ready to infect our creativity and self-worth.

But it's not true.

Sure, procrastination isn't a great state to be in. If you're procrastinating, it typically means that you're avoiding doing something you know you probably should be doing.

For some writers, procrastination is actually a useful tool. By waiting until it's almost too late to finish, the procrastinator creates a deliberate stress response, an ideal cognitive environment for laser focus and energy, exactly what's needed to get the work done efficiently.

For other writers, procrastination can be a symptom, and if we pay attention to what it's a symptom of, we can get to the heart of what's bothering us and what's preventing us from taking action.

So, what are you avoiding?

Why are you avoiding it?

Often, procrastination is rooted in fear.

We can all understand why we put off a task like cleaning a dirty bathroom—it's not a pleasant job. But why are you avoiding your writing, a job that you actually *want* to do?

Are you scared of not knowing what to write? Of writing badly?

Are you scared of someone reading what you write, or intend to write?

Are you writing the wrong project and scared to face what the right project might be?

Do not fear procrastination, but welcome it as a messenger and a useful tool. Heed the message, use the tool, and get to work.

WRITING AND PUBLISHING TECHNOLOGY

If you listen to the entire mass of writing and publishing advice out there, the message might sound like this:

"Want to write and publish a book? Do this: Write your book in the latest version of Scrivener, installed on a MacBook Pro, and make sure you can sync that to a smartphone so you can write on the go (and do you even know how to set up an Android phone to use Scrivener, because there's only an iOS app?). Use Evernote for your digital notes, and don't forget to sync that across devices too and your third-party cloud service. And learn to use ChatGPT as a writing assistant, even if you don't intend to work with it. And make sure you're using a penguin mouse and negative-tilt keyboard at a sit-stand desk, and even better, using Dragon software to dictate your book. When you're finished, convert the book into half a dozen e-book formats (if you don't use Vellum, you're already losing) and then upload that, together with your digital covers (did you get a Canva Pro subscription? You'll also need that for social media) into the various platforms and distributors, and it's best to have your print and e-books come out at the same time as your audiobook, and readers like an author-narrated audiobook the best, all the while using an automated mail service and at least one social media channel to talk to your fans, oh, and don't forget that self-hosted website. Oh, and have you ever considered serializing your

novels on subscription across the various platforms and then on Patreon? And podcasts are really the best marketing at the moment, and getting search-optimized videos on YouTube is a total must-have. What? You don't have a Patreon platform for your fans?! Have you thought about monetizing on Substack? Oh, you want to publish traditionally? Then you'll still have to do all that writing and marketing stuff with all that tech, and find an agent first (use social media for that), but best to do the marketing before you have an agent, so they can see you're really serious and have an established brand, and... and... and..."

STOP!

Take a deep breath.

Stop again.

To write a book, you need the most basic word processing software on a computer that turns on and reliably saves. Or, you need a pen and paper. That's all.

Write the book. And then figure out what you need or want to do next.

Can't figure it out on your own? Get one of the ten quadrillion people who love helping people with this stuff and ask them. Read their articles or watch their videos, or hire them to do it all for you. Just write the book first with whatever you already know how to use, or are happily willing to learn.

Then figure out what the next tool needs to do and use it with the same approach.

You don't have to do all the things, you don't have to use all the tools.

Keep it basic.

RESEARCH

Will I need to spend all of my writing time researching?

The prospect of researching for a book can be so huge and terrifying that it becomes impossible to manage.

How much research is enough?

What if I get something wrong, or miss a detail?

Some authors will research every single detail that goes into their work; others will research just enough to get a vibe for a situation and wing it from there.

Do as much research as you need to start writing, and research more along the way if necessary.

Beware holding off until you've researched everything before you start writing. There's *always* going to be something more to research, some deeper level to explore. Prioritize writing first.

Learn effective research methods.

Always check the validity of your sources, and cite your sources if it's appropriate for your work.

Even with careful study, all kinds of writers get all kinds of facts wrong. If this happens to you, apologize if appropriate, fix it, learn from your mistake, and know it's likely you and every other writer will make another one again. Move on, keep writing.

WRITING SLOW

This is a fear particular to indie publishing, where many believe that writers have to publish a gazillion books a year to have any chance of being successful.

It used to be a book a month, and then AI arrived and now people are engineering books in a day.

Do you really want to compete with that? Yes? Awesome. Go for it!

No? Breathe out and relax.

Yes, many authors churning out dozens of books do well financially, but consider the sustainability of such a model. Writing eighty hours a week has its cost. Do you want to pay that cost?

A book takes as long as it takes.

If your best books take four days or four weeks to create, then good for you. If it's four months, then embrace that, and if it's four years, then good for you. Write your way.

There are successful authors at every pace.

If you need further evidence that this is a subjective belief and nothing to fear, consider that many authors fear writing too fast.

WRITING FAST

Contrary to the fact that the publishing conversations want us to write faster (see previous chapter), there is also a widespread stigma attached to books written quickly.

Writers are supposed to labor over words, gently coax our masterpieces to life. Novels take years to write, not weeks or days! Of course, a book written at speed cannot be any good.

Because of this, many a writer who is a naturally rapid word slinger feels ashamed. We fear judgment from ourselves or others that because of the speed at which the story was born, its value is less.

This. Is. Rubbish.

We know it's subjective opinion because it exists alongside the contrary opinion that authors can only be successful if we write fast. Subjective opinion is not fact and can be safely ignored without fear.

Good books are written in as much time as it takes for the author to write the book. For some it's years. For others, months, weeks, days. AI now allows for hours.

If you're a rapid writer, own it. Be proud of that superpower and know that most writers wish they had it.

Also, writing fast is an excellent strategy to overcome

other fears that can keep a story as a work in progress for a long time.

Write fast. Outrun those fears that your writing is somehow wrong.

HARD WORK

Yes, writing is hard work. It's confusing and troubling and filled with doubt and sometimes feels like you'll never get it right. Until you do and then it gets easy again, and it's the best job in the world. Until it gets hard again. Repeat.

Writing *is* hard work, but every job has its hard parts.

Writing is hard, but it's also fun, and the good kind of weird, and entertaining, and enlivening, and rewarding, and playful, and satisfying.

Hard isn't a bad thing. And even when it does feel that way, you can do hard things.

NEVER WRITING THE NEXT BOOK

What if I've only got one book in me? Or one series? One idea?

You've poured everything into your first book, but when you get ready to write the next, you find you're out of ideas, out of energy, and fresh out of any way to make it happen. It's common, and for many writers it's a killing blow.

That doesn't have to be you.

There is always more writing, and there are always more ideas for your next work, whether that's your second, tenth, or hundredth book.

This doesn't mean that you need to hold back in that first novel. On the contrary. Pour it all out until you're empty.

Now, look at everything you've learned in life and craft. Take some time to refill, to refuel, to replenish. Your next book is waiting for you, with all that potential to be even better than the last.

ABANDONING A PROJECT

There's no reason to fear abandoning a project that's not working. Moving on can be creatively liberating and free you up to pursue more important or appropriate ideas.

That said, it's important that we writers finish more than we abandon.

Finish your story if only to prove to yourself that you can finish. Writing through the tricky middle bits is hard work. If you don't work through it regularly, it's always going to feel impossible. Finish your story to experience what finishing energy and finishing satisfaction feel like.

Finish the book so that you can look at it in the future and think, "This is actually a pretty neat story! What was I worried about?"

What is finishing this book worth?

What is the value in abandoning it?

If the value of dumping it is higher than the value of pushing on, then dump it.

No one is going to punish you for abandoning a project. No one is stopping you from returning to a previously abandoned project when the time is right.

The word "abandon" can also mean to set free.

Will abandoning this project let you live in creative abandon?

NEVER FINISHING

What if I never finish this book?

What if? Does it matter? Why aren't you finishing?

Might it be better to evaluate and consider abandoning? Or is it something to be conquered? An Everest to climb that will take you to the top of the world?

If you keep climbing, and in most cases, I suggest you do, it's just one word more. Fear of not finishing might push you forward. Or it might be the thing holding you still.

Whatever fear is holding on to you, the only way through it is word by word. Keep doing that until it's done.

WRITER'S BLOCK

Oh no! Do I have writer's block?

So many an author has thought, staring at their blank screen, the realization that they might be blocked hitting them with the same fear as if they've just found a symptom of some vile disease.

When diagnosing yourself with writer's block, consider whether you're truly blocked or whether you're just empty.

True writer's block is like procrastination. Most of the time, it's rooted in fear. Think of your writing like a blocked pipe, and fear as the muck holding everything back. What's stuck in your flow? Judgment? Failure? Honesty? Uncertainty? Impostor syndrome?

Other times, what feels like a block is actually that the flow has dried up. You're free of fear blocks, but nothing is coming out. Your creative well is dry. Or perhaps you're simply tired today. Replenish with rest, play and inspiration and watch the words flow again.

How do you know which manner of block you're dealing with?

Look inside.

You know the answer.

FIRST DRAFTS

How do I figure out where everything goes?

What if I don't get it right?

There are just so many words!

First drafts can be daunting and downright frightening. But they don't have to be.

Love writing them or hate them, for most writers, first drafts are always messy. That's the point. Whether they're preplanned or organically written, first drafts are rough sketches like any artist might draw up. Think of an architect's initial scribbled ideas. No one expects them to end up in the final construction, but they're critical in shaping that early stage of development.

It's the same for all kinds of writing, and all writers write their first drafts in the same way. Word by word. Eventually, there will be a big pile of words in the shape of a story.

If your first draft is riddled with problems (the case for most of us), fix it in revision. Revision is easier simply because the first draft was harder.

Hard is the nature of a first draft. If you know it's normal, you don't have to fear it.

Even with an outline, a first draft is still you venturing blind into unchartered territory. Feel that trepidation? It's an expected passenger on this journey, but never let it be your guide. Let fear tag along as you traverse the unknown led by inspiration, curiosity and dogged determination. When you write The End, even if the previous sixty thousand words are terribly messy, fear will dissolve and lie in waiting until the next first draft you begin, and you'll complete the epic journey together again.

LOW PRODUCTIVITY

Our society is obsessed with productivity. Everything has to be made, done, finished, made again, ever faster, ever more efficiently. We're told that even if we're slow, we still have to be consistently productive.

The core of all of this is so that we can more aptly serve the machine of capitalism. So that we can, as close as we can manage, live as machines.

Unfortunately, art got caught up in this industrialized madness as much as the rest of the world, perhaps the writing industry even more so.

Writers smash out words and flood out books. We hear stories of authors writing humongous numbers of books in relatively short amounts of time, and of the glorious piles of royalties this effort brings them.

If we write faster, we get more stories written, sure. That has great creative benefits and feelings of fulfillment and joy.

But the background message in a lot of author's heads is also that if we write faster, we get more money. If we write more, we'll be personally better and more *valuable*.

As such, productivity, or more precisely, low productivity, brings with it all kinds of fears.

If I don't write enough, I won't earn enough to support myself or my family.

If I don't write enough, I won't be able to keep up with the market, which means not only will I not make enough money, but I risk being lost in the crowd and irrelevant.

If I don't write enough, I am not enough.

High-velocity productivity for a writer can be excellent.

As said, we get more written, more ideas become a reality, and we get more creative exercise. In another chapter, we also looked at how writing fast can work to outrun the fearful criticisms of our inner editors. I'm not criticizing or separating myself from the dedicated pursuit of money or a long backlist. These are worthy goals and high productivity helps us reach them faster.

But we are not machines.

Write as much as you can while it still feels good, while it still works. And use machines to help you do that more efficiently if you want.

Yes, strive and achieve and feel good in that.

But remember, a massive word count, the length of your backlist, or the size of your bank balance is not a meter of your personal value. You're a human, you aren't assigned value metrics.

Productivity is relative. One author's efficient productivity is another author's recipe for burnout and the end of their author career.

Focus on producing yourself and your life well, not worrying about how quickly you're doing it.

WASTING WORDS

Writers often fear wasting words.

We fear writing something that will never be finished or published, or we fear writing something that will never make the final cut.

All those precious words, wasted.

Words are not a finite resource. So, what's the actual fear here?

It's typically a fear of wasting time and energy. These are the real finite resources.

But is it really a waste to write words that will never be used?

Every word you write teaches you something. You might learn how to be a better writer by deleting words you later identify as not being good enough or as being unnecessary. You might learn more about the subject you're actually writing about. You might learn what you don't want to write about by experiencing firsthand what it was like to write about it.

Learning is never a waste of time.

EXPERIMENTING

This entire book could be condensed into one solution. Experiment.

Whatever area of your writing life you're fearing, whatever the problem, experiment with a solution and see what happens.

But so many writers fear experimenting in itself.

We face a question.

Should this story be in first or third person?

What should this character do next?

Will this genre sell?

Will this idea fit into this market trend?

Is it better to write in the morning or night?

Should I write in Scrivener?

Should I edit as I write, or fast draft?

Should I write shorter chapters? Should I write a split POV?

What if I get it all wrong?

We fear doing it one way because we fear getting it wrong. We fear not knowing we've gotten it wrong until someone tells us so. We fear wasting time, wasting energy.

But taking that time, using that creative energy and experimenting is the only way to know for sure what does work for you. It's the only way to put fear in the back seat for good.

Whatever the question, whatever the fear, just try one way and see what happens.

Keep your mind in this experimental mindset, and fear doesn't stand a chance.

There is no wrong way to experiment.

PART FIVE
EDITING

FINDING HELP

So, you've written a book and need the eyes of an early reader to help you pull it into the best shape it can be.

For some writers, this is an easy step and they know just who to call upon.

For others, finding that supportive person is not so easy, and this can be scary. Who will be the right person? And how do you find those people in the first place?

Start in your immediate life. A friend or family member. This only works if showing your work to your close people isn't a fear in itself. Consider also whether this person will tell you everything is wonderful because they love you. That's nice, but not helpful.

Go wider. A local or online writer's group? Social media?

Go wider still. Search up professional beta readers. Join a critique circle and offer a reciprocal arrangement. Go to editor directories, read qualifications and reviews.

Find a reader and or an editor who understands your genre. Trust your gut on whether they will be a good match for you and your book. Get them to edit a sample of your work. Most freelance editors offer this service. If it turns out they're not a good match, consider why, and start the search over again.

There is an entire industry of people whose job it is to help authors. Don't be scared. Get amongst it.

PROFESSIONAL CRITICISM

You finish a book. It's exciting and relieving, but you're still not ready to exhale yet. You pass your book over to a beta reader or a critique partner or editor and the fear grips in your belly.

What if it's not good?

What if I have to rewrite the whole thing?

What if they hate it and rip it to shreds?

It's okay. Breathe out. It's daunting but nothing to truly fear.
Start by considering what role this early reader has.
A beta reader's job is to tell you if they liked the book, if it's readable, and perhaps why or why not.
A critique reader's job is to find mistakes and focus on the negative.
An editor's job is both of those things and to help you fix them.
You do not have to employ any of these early readers if you choose not to. A caveat goes for editors, who are a neces-

sity for both traditional and independently published authors in different ways.

A beta reader offers an opinion. A critique, too, is an opinion. You can choose whether it's worth listening to.

Consider too the expertise of these early readers. Perhaps only the professional editor is truly worth listening to. That too is up to you.

We employ these readers to help us. No one is out to destroy your work or your creative spirit. Even the most misguided and critical critique reader is trying to improve your work, whether or not you think it needs improving. It's not an insult. It's a suggestion and usually comes from a good place.

If it takes a few typo fixes to improve your book, good for you.

If it takes an entire rewrite, good for you. Get to work and make it a better book.

FIXING THE FIRST DRAFT

You've finished a first draft and you're staring at an enormous pile of words and not all of them are even in the right order. There are typos everywhere, sentences that don't make sense, dialogue that reads like gibberish, and plot holes big enough to sink an entire universe into.

How on earth are you going to fix this mess and turn it into a real book?

Sure, tackling that job is terrifying! But only if you consider it in its entirety. Be smart about it.

Revising a messy first draft happens just like that first draft was written, piece by piece.

But revision happens in reverse of drafting. Instead of going word by word, tackle the bigger things first, plot structure and so on, and save the sentence-level edits for last. These macro-level elements are easier to hold on to, and once you've got them in place, they provide a firmer footing on which to establish the rest, word by word.

PART SIX
PUBLISHING AND THE WRITING BUSINESS

AUTHENTICITY

Authenticity is an annoying buzzword. It's important, but it's become incredibly confusing.

We're told we must have it. So writers fear not having it. Oftentimes, this is because we have no idea what anyone actually means when they say "be authentic."

Authenticity means being real, honest, and true. This isn't a bad thing. Don't lie. Don't fake. It's an honorable value to live by.

But when we get into the online culture, or any culture where we're putting a product or a piece of art into the world —and this includes writing—the idea of authenticity gets confusing and scary.

Am I being authentic enough?

Do I have to reveal everything about myself and my private life?

Is that other person being authentic? Can I trust them? Can they trust me?

In the pursuit of authenticity, authenticity has become inauthentic. Hashtag Authenticity. Authenticity has become a style, an aesthetic and a commodity, but our culture is still pretending it's a value. And that's why it's scary.

In order to stop fearing authenticity, let's give it another name.

Integrity. Honesty.

You don't need to put every detail of your life out into the world or into your writing. Curate your truth to the level you're comfortable with and it will still have honest integrity.

WRITING TO MARKET

Writing to market became a widespread concept about ten years ago in the independent author community. The idea is that an author finds a category (typically on the Amazon Kindle store) that has a solid number of readers but not a huge saturation of books and writes in that niche.

Some authors love this strategy and do very well. Other authors fear the very concept of writing to market.

It's selling out.

It's inauthentic.

It compromises a writer's creativity.

Writing to market doesn't need to be feared. There are different ways to approach it so that it always fits your creative sensibilities, so that you never sell out, so that you're always authentic.

First, you can ignore markets entirely and write whatever you want, however you want, whenever you want.

Alternatively, understand that writing to market does not insist that you write something you're not interested in writing. Find the crossover between your creative passion and the reading passion of certain readers. Authors sometimes call this "writing to reader," which has a far less imposing sense to it.

Yes, some writers essentially ghostwrite for themselves, writing to market for the sake of the market only. Some writers love this work and it's just another way to do it.

Write the book you want to write, always. If there's a particular readership for that style book already, then wonderful.

Don't forget that markets change. They fade, they emerge. Authors can and have intentionally engineered new markets to fit the stories they want to tell.

NOT USING SOCIAL MEDIA

Ten years ago, it was unfathomable to think that anyone could exist without having a social media presence. Okay, that's an exaggeration, but it was certainly spouted for any business, including authors, that social media was a must-have.

This wasn't true then, and it's not true now. The difference is that now we're seeing how these platforms work and what they really do for an author, and also how damaging they can be for anyone.

Social media is what you make it. Some writers do tremendously well using socials to connect with readers and other authors and sell a lot of books. Many authors do not. Many authors don't even like using social media. Perhaps it's a hangover from the last decade of being told it's a must-have, but many authors are afraid not to use it for fear of missing out on its advantages.

There is a lot to be gained for yourself and your writing by not using social media at all. Many authors have vibrant and prosperous writing lives without it. You can be one of those authors too, if you choose to be.

USING SOCIAL MEDIA

For some writers, social media is a necessary part of their authoring process, whether that's for writing itself or promotion of their books. For others, social media is a terrifying landscape of misery and corruption.

Like any other tool, social media can be used for good, and those writers leaning toward the second camp need not fear its use.

Social media can enable connection and promotion, if that's how you choose to use it. It can enable creative inspiration.

You do not have to use social media in the way that social media tells you to use social media. You might not have control over your content on these platforms, but you have control over how much and to what purposes you engage with this technology.

Try it out. See what it feels like. If you're already on, try using it in different ways and find a way that suits you. If you don't like it, then move away. That's a valid choice too.

JUDGMENT

It's normal and human to fear judgment in anything, particularly something so expressive as writing.

We fear judgment because we usually think of it as a negative thing. To be judged harshly is to be rejected, and in our primeval nervous systems, rejection is a threat to our very lives.

Judgment, good or bad, is an unavoidable part of the job of a publishing writer. We put our words out into the world for readers to consume, and judgment, good or bad, occurs automatically in that consumption.

Naturally, we want this to be a good judgment, but reality dictates it won't always be that way.

Not everyone is going to like your book. Do you like every book you've ever read? Of course not. Accept that someone won't like your work and move on; write another book and accept that someone won't like that one either.

If you must listen to judgments of your work, focus on the people that *do* like it. But remember, their opinion is just as subjective as the other side of the judgment coin.

Your job is to write and serve yourself first. Judgment belongs to the readers, so just let them get on with it while you do your job.

DEADLINES

What if I miss the deadline?

I will disappoint people. I will disappoint myself. I will lose my publishing opportunity. I will be a failure.

Deadlines are useless for some authors, and completely necessary for others. The necessity of a deadline might be external, working with traditional publishers, cowriting and the like, situations where other people are relying on your work so they can do theirs.

Or a deadline can be internally self-imposed. You set yourself a date to finish a task so that you can fit it into a goal system, or the rest of your life.

Many authors need a deadline as a pressure switch to keep them motivated, keep them working, getting the words done.

Many authors don't set deadlines and do just fine.

If deadlines bother you for whatever reason, consider if you *need* to set them. Indie authors do not need deadlines. Many set them—preorder dates, preannounced released dates, or other self-imposed finish lines—but many of us just work until it's done, crossing the finish line when we get there.

If you do truly require deadlines, and you're not an author who works well under them, then consider the following options.

Negotiate the deadline far in advance, allowing more time than you realistically need.

If you're under the pressure of a deadline about to fall and you're not ready to meet it, consider what's really at stake.

What is the worst thing that will happen if you don't meet it?

Can you negotiate for more time? What is the worst thing that will happen if you ask?

Is the stress of not meeting the deadline affecting your work, or worse, your health, in a negative way? What's worth more? Choose a side.

Or are you simply underestimating yourself or your capacity for focus, and perhaps forgetting that the stress of a looming deadline is a necessary element of your writing process?

If you do need to change a deadline for any reason, chances are that worst outcome will not mean your death or eternal social ostracism.

EXTERNAL EXPECTATIONS

What if I can't live up to other people's expectations of me?

What if I want to write something different from what readers expect?

This fear can paralyze a writer's productivity and creativity. But it's actually a good place to find yourself in.

If readers have expectations of your work, it means you have readers. You've attracted people, drawn them in, and they want more of what you have to offer. Isn't that every publishing writer's goal?

But what if you want to change what you offer?

What if you fear you cannot repeat whatever drew readers to you?

If you want to change your offering, write in a different style, a different genre, then change. Perhaps go back to your former style after a creative exploration. Or continue on the new path with your new offerings. You might bring along those same readers, or you might attract new readers. All the fearful "What ifs...?" attached to this situation aren't worth shackling your creativity for.

For the second, the only way to tell if you can repeat the effect of your initial offerings is to write, publish, and see what happens.

Once again, as with so many writers' fears, the calm comes in the writing.

NOT BEING TAKEN SERIOUSLY

What does it mean *not* to be taken seriously as a writer?

Not to be respected? To have people believe you cannot write? To have people believe you cannot sell a book?

What does it mean to be taken seriously as a writer?

To write? To publish? To sell? To connect?

Before you let a fear of not being taken seriously knock you down, consider what it actually means to be taken seriously or not. Now decide if it even matters. Isn't this just another subjective external opinion?

Write, read, learn, publish, connect. Take yourself seriously, take the work seriously. And then lighten up about the whole writing world. Remember how to play and not take yourself or the writing so seriously.

PLATFORM

This is one of those notions that has many a writer quivering in their inkwells.

Building a platform is marketer speak for creating a place, usually online, where readers can find your work.

At the very least, it's a bookstore page like your Amazon author profile. A step up might look like a static author website. One up from there, it's a mailing list, or a social media presence. At most, it's a complex website with direct sales, an ongoing blog, millions of social media posts, podcasts, subscriptions, video channels, and…

STOP!

What do you feel most comfortable with? A basic landing page and nothing more? Then that's the right platform for you. A multimedia extravaganza? Then go for it (as long as you're still getting the books written and not redesigning your website or living on social media all day). You can start at the bottom and move up, adding to your platform as you go, subtracting as you learn what you want and don't.

The fear of platform stems from the fear of being seen, of being judged, of being misunderstood, of doing it all wrong. Like the rest of your writing world, do it on your terms, the way that feels right, the way that works for you, and leave the external opinions to the people who are having them.

DISORGANIZATION

It's a wonderful thing that we can connect with so many other authors and listen to them talk about their processes. But…

That author does it so much better than I do.

That author is so much more organized than I am.

That author is so much more professional than I am. Look at their spreadsheets! Their production schedules!

I'm a hack. Is there even any point?

These fears from comparison are fears of self-value, a worry that you're doing it all wrong and are therefore holding yourself back.
So, you try all the different things.
The spreadsheets and the bullet journals and the production schedules, preorders, scheduled posts, whatever the case may be. You didn't know what a Kanban board was yesterday, but now you're convinced it's the thing that will solve all your problems. But it doesn't work, you just keep on coming back to your ways that look disheveled in comparison.

Does your process work?

Does your organization system, or lack thereof, get your books written? Does it get all the other work done?

Sure, your system might stand some tweaking, fine-tuning, or even a total overhaul complete with color coded Post-its and a mood board for every book, but only if that's what *you* need. There's no need to turn your process upside down because someone else has more spreadsheets than you or their Post-its are color coded. Other writers are getting the job done with just as much seemingly unprofessional disorganization, and you can listen to those voices too.

BEING COMPARED TO OTHERS

Comparisonitis is a pop-psych fear syndrome we all know well. It's when we compare ourselves in whatever context to other writers and fear that we're lacking.

It can be a heavy burden for many authors.

How do we handle it?

The impulse advice is to ignore it. But comparison is hard-wired into our primeval nerves. How do we know if we belong to the pack without comparing ourselves to others? So instead try accepting that it's there and it's normal, and carry on.

Remember yourself. Your unique work, your unique visions, voices, and methods of writing.

This is the only thing to measure. If it's serving us, if we're working with honest integrity, doing our best at any given moment and remembering that our best yesterday might be different to our best today and tomorrow, then that's the only reference point we need.

LOSING CREATIVE CONTROL

When we first start out on the writing journey, it's just us, the ideas, and the words. We dream of holding up our finished books and offering them to the world.

A strong appeal of independent publishing is that we have almost total control over every aspect of the writing and publishing. We get to decide what's in the book and what the book looks like. Traditionally published authors do not have this luxury, at least to the same degree, and for many, it's a fear.

What if they change my story too much?

What if they compromise my vision?

It's a fear of losing creative control.
What's the solution?
Consider a compromise. Can you find a happy middle ground that suits everyone? If it's not possible, try to see the other side's reasons for the changes, or state your own and try to change their perspective. If that still doesn't work, and you're still fearing you've been creatively compromised and can't get through it, then ask yourself why you're pursuing

traditional publishing. If total creative autonomy is really that important to you, then consider the indie model.

Self-publishing cannot offer absolute creative independence, not if we want to sell our books, at least. We're still subject to the whims of the markets, the restrictions of the distributors, and the like. We all need to find a middle ground on this. Fortunately for the indie author, that middle ground is far more flexible than traditional publishing can ever allow.

OFFENDING THE SUBJECT

If you are writing about other people and other people's lives, in a fictional or factual context, there is a very real chance that person will not like what you've written.

It could result in conflict, a simple argument or something worse. At the extreme end of this scenario, it can result in the offended party taking legal action. Scary stuff.

The best way around this fear is to try not to find yourself in this situation.

Do you really need to write about this other person?

If you truly want to write about someone else, get their permission. Subject them to an accurate and fair representation, and get their (or their representative's) opinions on what is accurate and fair. If this isn't possible, get someone else's opinion. Seek your own legal advice before anything goes public.

Alternatively, use this person as base inspiration for your subject, but fictionalize them. This will need more than a simple name change. Perhaps only use one element of their story, or twist even that one element. Every author uses real people for inspiration to some degree. Most of us make that person unrecognizable but still find satisfaction in bringing that real person to the page.

If we're not talking about actual libel and defamation legal battles and someone is just annoyed with you, it might be a case of simply getting comfortable with their discomfort. If you have made a fair, honest representation of your subject, you have external opinion backing that up, and your subject still gets offended, it might not be your problem. Stand in the courage of your own conviction.

OFFENDING READERS

It's a given that not everyone will enjoy what we write. Every book has critical reviews, after all. But what if that displeasure comes in the form of complete offense?

This differs from a fear of someone you're specifically writing about being offended. This is a fear that your general content will cause offense to a general readership.

Are you writing deliberately offensive material? There are a few fringe genres that set out to unsettle and offend some aspect of the wider culture. I am not here referring to blatantly toxic content such as racism, sexism, harmful sexual deviancies, hate speech, promoting crime, and the like, nor promoting or condoning such content (if you're this writer, then please stop!). Instead, I refer to genres like erotica and steamy kink romance, or horror, places were conventional boundaries are deliberately pushed in safe ways.

Readers in these genres are looking for that experience, to intentionally witness those boundaries being pushed, and therefore, aren't offended. Other readers come to these genres specifically looking to be offended and to let the world know about their outrage. This latter group are not your readers, so you can safely disregard their opinions and get back to work. Authors in these genres typically accept this as part of the job.

Writing in conventional genres still has the potential to cause offense, but this is still nothing to be feared. As long as you're not deliberately setting out to offend with the kinds of toxic content referenced above, then it's not in your control what a reader might find offensive. If it's your truth, if it's fair and accurate and not toxic, promoting or intending hurt, then the offense is entirely subjective, and it's safe and acceptable for you to keep on writing.

If you do cause offense, unintentionally or otherwise, and then retrospectively see how you might have handled things better, apologize with sincerity, restate your position, and move on, having learned a lesson.

CONTROVERSY

A fear of writing controversy isn't quite the same as a fear of offending a subject or reader.

A fear of writing controversy is having something to say about a particular subject you know some people will be challenged by. It could be offense, it could be disagreement.

How will you handle these complaints?

Most of us don't truly want to upset other people, but there are certain situations where that upset is warranted and even necessary. All cases of positive social change are controversial.

If you're fearing controversy, then you're likely not writing intentionally inflammatory content with the intention to hurt. You've got something to say but are worried about attracting a negative reaction.

If that something you have to say is something you believe in, if it's fair and true, if it's not toxic (racism, sexism, criminal, hate, harmful sexual deviance, etc.), if it's not actively going to harm people or promote harm, then you are allowed to state your position.

Consider the other side.

Situate your opinions in fairness and factual accuracy.

You will still rattle people and be prepared to accept those opinions gracefully. If those opinions manage to change your position in any way, own that too, apologize if necessary, alter your position, and demonstrate what a reasonable and enlightened person looks like.

Keep writing.

PIRACY

Piracy is a fact of the internet.

If you publish your book in any digital form, your book will likely be pirated.

Many authors rail against this, and some authors resist digital publishing or cover their e-books in layers of antipiracy measures in an attempt to control the issue.

You can't control the issue. No one can. Governments try, but pirate sites are always ten steps ahead.

So stop worrying about it.

Sure, if you see your book pirated, issue a notice against it, but it will not stop piracy.

Switch on antipiracy measures like digital rights management if it makes you feel better, but remember that these technologies often make it hard for legitimate readers to access your books on various devices.

Change your mindset about piracy.

Pirates don't buy books, so you aren't losing any potential sales income, but you are reaching new readers. Accept a pirate reader as a compliment and get back to focusing on legal readers who actually want to give you their money for your stories.

NO MONEY

When we look to the loudest writing voices, and this is particularly true of indie authors, it's often those making considerable bank that most of us pay attention to.

We emulate their strategies, dream of ourselves hitting and surpassing those six figures, and then wind up disappointed and disillusioned that we didn't get there, fearing we never will.

Many authors let the fear of not making any money force them to give up.

Many authors let the fear of not making any money prevent them from ever starting.

Money, or the lack thereof, is fertile soil for impostor syndrome and comparisonitis and all kinds of fears of failure, judgment, and expectations.

While there are certainly some authors who have earned considerable amounts from their writing, most writers do not come to this work with riches in mind. Like any field, wealth is possible, but not everyone gets there.

Still, there is no reason to assume authors are doomed to poverty.

The reality for most publishing writers is in the middle. Earning money is possible, even likely if you're making all the best moves in smart ways, doing your research and working as a businessperson. Will you make millions? Probably not, but even the people who do will tell you that that's not really up to them either. Publishing is a gamble.

If you want work with a guaranteed way of earning a reliable, stable income, or far-flung riches, then get a different job.

Are you really here only for the money?

DISCOVERABILITY

Discoverability is arguably the most difficult part of a writing career.

You can write an amazing book, work with all the best beta readers and editors, and show off an amazing cover, but if the world doesn't see your book, there are no readers. If there are no readers, there is no career. A lot is riding on discoverability, so it's no wonder it conjures fear in many writers.

Embracing agency is one way to calm fear. You can't control the reading market, but there are some actions you can take to give yourself a better chance to be seen and read.

Different authors have different tactics, and marketing strategies are as unique to authors as writing styles. Find the one, or the multiple, that suits your personality, your lifestyle, as well as the one that attracts readers at the same time, and follow that with the assuredness that you're doing all you can. The rest is up to a trickster god playing in a fractured universe built on chaos. Or at least that's how the publishing world seems most of the time.

As you're working to get readers into your pages, remember also that no writers need to attract the whole market. Not even the majority of a single genre's readership. A tiny percentage will work just fine.

TRENDS

Some writers find remarkable success in following or even predicting market trends and adapting their writing accordingly. It might be a trending genre market or niche, a trope, or a publishing platform or strategy.

Many authors see this success and, understandably impressed, attempt to ride trends, but they fall short. Others see it and already know it's not their style.

Fear lurks on both sides. Comparisonitis screams loudly. Ultimately a fear of shifting trends is a fear of failure and a fear of missing out. It's a fear of not being able to work enough, or as well as needed, to operate in this way, and deeper in that, we go back to the fear of failure.

I don't have what it takes to catch a trend. I'm not good enough and am doomed.

I will never be able to keep up and I'll miss all the hot trends.

I'm not good enough and am doomed.

If these are your fears, remember that most authors don't

work like this. The writers who do find success in chasing trends are typically outliers.

Many writers find amazing success in sticking with what they like to write, following their curiosity, and letting market trends move by unnoticed.

You get to decide which side you want to play on.

INTELLECTUAL THEFT

What if someone steals my ideas?

It comes up in every circle of fledgling authors.

Some authors tell no one of their ideas for fear of another grabbing it and stealing their book from under them. Some authors will not publish digitally for fear this will more easily enable plagiarism.

Intellectual theft is a real thing and can be a problem. This is even more true in the age of AI, as we've now also got the machines coming for our words. But it's seldom anything we need to fear.

Plagiarism is not to be condoned. There is a difference between someone stealing your words and another author working from the same ideas and concepts. There is also a difference between plagiarism and having your words scraped to fuel a generative AI bot.

Having your work scraped by AI isn't plagiarism. Your exact writing is not going to be spat out by ChatGPT. It's an ethical minefield, though, and we simply don't know at this stage how it will work. It's a matter to consider, and perhaps even raise concern over, but again, it's nothing to fear.

Plagiarism happens, and even if it happens explicitly to

your work, there's no need to fear it. There are legal measures to protect your rights. There are steps to take. Plagiarists rarely win at their game.

And what if someone steals your idea? We're not talking about your actual prose here, but the idea you used to build your story.

It's not going to take away from your story. It might even enhance it.

Ideas are cheap, maybe even more so in the age of generative AI. Ideas are everywhere. The value of an idea comes in its execution. Give ten writers (and even a chatbot) the same idea, and you're going to end up with ten completely different and unique stories.

If it makes you comfortable, hold your ideas to your chest in dark secret caves. Or perhaps consider how much richer that idea might become if you share it and hear others' thoughts. Combination of disparate ideas is, after all, what creative thinking is all about.

REJECTION

Fearing rejection in writing is like fearing words—it's just a part of the job.

If you're submitting to traditional marketplaces, you will get rejected more than you're accepted.

What if I can't find an agent?

What if I can't find a publisher?

Some authors don't want to independently publish their books, for many reasons, but in the pursuit of traditional publishing come up against these two fears.

So, what if?

Publishers and agents *want* to work with writers. They *need* writers. Without the writer there is no publishing.

But there are a lot of writers and even more books.

What does it mean if a writer has trouble finding a publisher or agent?

That their writing isn't good enough to be represented?
Perhaps.

That the agent or publisher is already fully booked?
Perhaps.

That the particular agent or publisher isn't suited to or interested in that particular type of writing, regardless of how good it is?

Perhaps.

The list is long, but what it doesn't mean is that the writer is a failure in any sense.

A writer having difficulty landing an agent or publisher is not a failure. The writer is just unpublished or unrepresented by that particular agent or publisher. They can try another, and another.

Then, if their attempts are still coming up empty, consider the reasons said author doesn't want to independently publish.

But even indies aren't immune to rejection. For the self-published author, rejection comes in the form of no sales and negative reviews (which happens for trad authors too).

Rejection is just the way we sort through the chaff and make sure our words hit the right readers. Rejection is also a way of figuring out what's wrong with a piece of writing (maybe only helpful if rejection also comes with feedback).

Don't fear rejection—embrace it. If you're rejected, it means you've put your writing into the world. Many new authors don't even make it this far. You've taken the first step, now learn and keep going.

NOT SELLING

What if my book doesn't sell?

What if my book doesn't sell enough?

Not selling books is a sub-fear of the fear of failure, but where is this fear coming from? Is it financial? Is it about others' opinions and expectations? Is it about comparisons? Is it all of the above or something else?

Ultimately, not selling is a reality. Sometimes even good books don't sell, or don't sell well, or don't sell as expected or hoped. It could be a discoverability factor. It could be that it just isn't the right time in the wider culture. It could be that the book itself isn't that great. It could be luck.

The only way to stop fearing not selling is to see if your book will sell. And the only way to see if a book will sell is to write and publish it.

Sales aren't the only reward metric of writing in a qualitative or quantitative sense, so focus on those rewards and values that you can more readily predict and rely on. Like the fulfillment of writing in itself, like showing up to the page. If your book doesn't sell, keep trying different sales strategies, and in the meantime, write another one.

NEGATIVE FEEDBACK

Every writer will experience some form of negative feedback.

For many, it's a source of fear. While it might not be enough to stop you from writing, it's a truth that it stops many a writer from publishing or sharing their work in any other way.

Writing is a lot of things, and some of those things are deeply personal, only between the writer and their page. But at its core, writing is communication, a conversation, and that communication needs to happen between people.

Writing wants to be shared. We all want people to love our work, but fearing the reality of the potential opposite to the point of publishing paralysis stops anyone from liking your work too.

We can't stop negative feedback. But we can take measures so that it doesn't hurt, so that it's nothing to fear.

Your writing is not going to appeal to everyone, so don't even bother putting your energy into bad reviews. They sting, but consider them with perspective and focus on the positive. Or ignore all reviews, good and bad.

What about negativity from early readers? You always have the option of ignoring negative feedback from beta readers and critique partners and doing whatever you want. That said, if a few readers give you the same negative feedback, it's likely worth listening to.

Negative feedback is just opinion. And opinion is optional.

THE MARKET

The market, as a concept, can seem like some uncontrollable, tyrannical, enigmatic force that only Amazon algorithm coders working in their top-secret underground lairs understand. It's terrifying!

There's only one element of truth in that picture—the publishing market is uncontrollable (but I wouldn't be surprised if Amazon's algorithms really are designed in top-secret underground lairs, potentially by coders wearing ominous cloaks).

The market is organic and dynamic. It ebbs and flows unpredictably. Not even major publishers (or Amazon coders) know how it will swing next. So why waste your time and energy fearing something that has less predictability than the weather in spring? We can see what to expect to a degree, but unexpected, wild, and life-changing twists happen.

Sure, study the market. Learn its current conventions, past patterns and trends. If you choose to write in an attempt to match those patterns, then do so proudly, boldly, but also with the knowledge that it's still a gamble.

Or forget the market and write what you want, rested in the knowledge that many successful authors do just that, and many of them have gone on to define what the rest of us are calling "the market."

The market is made by readers and writers, and we're all just people liking stuff to read and liking stuff to write. There's nothing scary about that.

SHARING YOUR WRITING

How many reasons are there that a writer might fear sharing their writing?

Many of them are explored in other chapters in this book. Fear of being misunderstood, of negative feedback, of not getting the publisher or agent or book sales that you hope for.

Ultimately, a fear of sharing our writing comes down to feeling scared because we think we're unworthy, or we fear others thinking we're unworthy.

To get beyond this fear, there needs to be a separation of author and work, as impossible as it seems at times to draw yourself away from the thing that comes out of your deepest, most intimate spaces.

A comment, good or bad, is on the work, not your value as a person.

If you fear the potential of the negative reaction happening, then by protecting yourself from that by not sharing, you're also preventing the potential of a positive from ever becoming real.

Writing is for reading and humans are for connecting.

Share your work and make a connection. It gets easier.

TRADITIONAL PUBLISHING

Traditional publishing is a big scary industry that's only out to steal your words and rip you off with limiting contracts that will bind you to the grave and beyond.

Traditional publishing is a fickle business that's too competitive and unpredictable to ever find lasting success in, and the rejection of even trying to break into it will probably wear you down before you even get a chance to end up in the remainders bin.

Traditional publishing is terrifying!

This is a bleak view, and for the record, it's not my actual opinion. It's a hyperbolic representation of the spirit of why many authors fear traditional publishing.

Yes, trad publishing is a difficult business. Yes, many authors find trouble, and even more authors don't even get in the front door to begin with.

But that doesn't mean it's a hellscape to be avoided.

Traditional publishing launches many wonderfully successful writing careers. Trad publishers get millions of books into the hands of millions of readers every day, and often in such ways that it allows the writers to focus on their favorite part of the industry—the writing.

Traditional publishing is not for everyone, but it is for

many, and to find out if you're one of those many just takes experimentation and perseverance. It's hard work. But if you truly feared hard work you wouldn't be a writer.

Remember too that it doesn't have to be an either-or equation. Traditional publishing might be the right place for an author at one time in their life, or for one book, and another route might be the best option at another, or simultaneously. It might seem like traditional publishing makes up all the rules to the game, but you get to decide how or even if you want to play.

INDEPENDENT PUBLISHING

The most common arguments against indie publishing I hear are from writers who:

Fear marketing themselves;

Fear the amount of work involved;

Fear it's the second-best option;

Fear that it's not "real" publishing.

All writing is hard work.

Every published writer, indie or otherwise, needs to market their own work and their brand.

Indie publishing certainly makes very real careers out of very real books, and for many writers, it's the number one choice.

There doesn't need to be this huge distinction between traditional and independent publishing. The core goal of both sides is the same: to connect writer with reader by way of a book.

With indie publishing, we let the readers decide if that book is the best connection for them.

If indie publishing sparks a curiosity, then follow it. If it doesn't, don't. Like just about everything else in the writing life, it's up to you and how you want to create.

MARKETING

This is the aspect of being a published author that scares writers the most. I believe that's because marketing is misunderstood, or ignored and rejected before a misunderstanding can even take place.

Marketing is not yelling out about how great you and your books are. Endless posts, expensive ads, publicity campaigns, and a bunch of other over-the-top pitching methods are what many a writer runs away from marketing in fear of.

This kind of marketing contains many fears. Fears of annoying readers, fears of rejection, fears of your work not even being worth the effort to begin with.

But marketing doesn't have to be like this, nor *should* it be like this.

What is marketing?

Showing your books to people who like books.

Redefine it.

Marketing is letting potential readers see that your book exists. And the best marketing is doing it in a way that lets a reader see you're a real person looking to connect with another real person and offering to share something valuable. It's telling a story about the author who wrote the book and why the reader will like it, and telling that story in a creative way. Sounds like exactly the thing a writer would enjoy, right?

Some writers do all this with paid ads. Some don't.

Some writers do it with email newsletters. Some don't.

Some writers do it with podcasts, social media, YouTube, blogging, in-person events, and so many other things. Some don't.

You tell your stories in the way that suits you best. So now tell the story of how that story came to be and who you wrote it for in the same way. There's nothing to fear about telling that story.

MISSING AN OPPORTUNITY

FOMO, the kids are calling it. The Fear of Missing Out.

You know if it's got a clever acronym and a vastly populated Instagram hashtag, it has to be a ubiquitous concept.

While we are social creatures, humans aren't designed to live as a whole-world society—which is what the internet has enabled. All of this mega-level hyperconnection has its benefits, absolutely. But FOMO is one of the downsides. We see the whole world in a never-ending, always-churning feed. We see all these people doing interesting things and seizing remarkable opportunities and we want it too. All of it. And because it all feels so within reach, there's no reason why we can't have every opportunity available to us.

This is really scary.

We know we have options, but what if the one we choose isn't the best one, or there's another one just as good that we want too? What are we leaving on the table?

For writers, FOMO could mean missing out on the chance to publish in a hot trend or a format, or missing out on an award, a grant, or an agent, missing out on the next technological boom, the opportunity to take a workshop, to go on a retreat, the chance to finish our book or all the books we want to write. It's a fear of missing out on anything, and more specifically it's a fear of missing out on everything.

But here's why it makes no sense.

You *will* miss out. We all do. We simply can't have or do everything!

But we can have and do a lot, and we can make choices that suit our needs, ourselves and our lives. And we can revel in those choices.

We might still carry the fear of missing an opportunity, but this is one of those irritating cases where we just have to carry the fear along with us while we get on with more important things.

Go deep into the experiences you do choose and let the rest of the world do what they're doing, and consider yourself lucky you're not exhausted chasing every little thing that could be great. It's called JOMO. The Joy of Missing Out.

PUBLIC SPEAKING

Writers aren't the only folks afraid of public speaking. It ranks as one of the most common fears people have in general.

For writers, though, it might have a few more scary edges.

Public speaking for writers often involves talking about our work, or reading our work out loud. Sure, stand up in front of a crowd and offer your innermost self. That doesn't sound terrifying at all!

We fear public speaking for the same reasons that we have impostor syndrome or a fear of criticism. Because we're wired to fit in. If we don't fit in with the pack, we're left out in the cold, alone and defenseless. Or so our primitive brains perceive.

Public speaking adds an extra dimension to that threat because we stand up before the pack and ask for the group's attention. We want them to focus on us, and that makes it feel more likely that they'll see our flaws, see how we don't fit, and kick us out into the wilds.

But is that really going to happen? Of course not (unless you're attending some unusually savage writer events).

I'm not sure anyone truly conquers a fear of public speaking. I believe the fears get reframed. Fear and excitement have the same physical responses, after all; it's just the stories we attach to them that make them mean different things.

How do we make that mindset shift? Consult one of the millions of resources available on the fear of public speaking and remember that the fact that there are so many resources available, even some specifically written for writers, is proof that you're not alone in this.

Audiences are made up of people, and people, mostly, are okay and don't actually want to hurt you. They're in your audience, after all, so there's a good chance they sincerely *do* want to hear what you have to say.

BECOMING OBSOLETE

You know that saying about death and taxes. Well, not everyone pays taxes, but everything does change, and everything we do will one day pass, including ourselves.

But it can be hard, even frightening, to think about our writing like this. Some stories have lasted thousands of years, after all. And many more outlive their authors, maintaining relevance across generations, if not eternity.

But many more still fall away, forgotten.

For some authors the very prospect of this is an unsettling fear. If our books are forgotten, then so are we.

This fear of becoming obsolete need not even extend beyond generations.

Genres rise to the top of the bestseller charts at breakneck speed, and suddenly a certain type of book is the only thing anyone's talking about. And then, there's a new hot thing and the last hot thing is now cold and forgotten.

No one can truly predict a market trend.

No one can know what will remain in the cultural consciousness or what will fade.

So just write your story.

Those stories that do last generations and longer have things in common. They deal in universal truths and connective human experiences. This isn't to say we all have to write lofty philosophical literary fiction or risk obsolescence. Just write a story, in any genre, about something bigger than all of us and still something so small as to be contained in every one of us.

Simple, right? Of course it's not. So just write your story. Any story you like.

The effect of you doing so will live inside your body, color your life, and positively affect everyone around you in this generation and the next. That's the stuff that really lasts.

PART SEVEN
LIFESTYLE

IT'S TOO LATE

There's only one phase of life you'll ever find yourself in when it's too late to start writing.

You already know what the bleak answer to that is.

Memento mori.

Today is not too late, but tomorrow might be.

The same goes for writing as it does for that tree proverb. The best time to start writing was twenty years ago. The next best time to start is now.

IT'S TOO SOON

Writers are supposed to be these wizened souls who impart their life-learned knowledge with well-wrought words. Right?

What could a young person have to teach us about the world?

I'm too young to be taken seriously.

Or perhaps you've got the years stacked behind you in number but fear you lack the life experience to write a worthy word.

Yes, the best writing comes from a lived life, but the length of that life, or the experience within, doesn't mean the stories aren't worth telling. Even children have something to say about the world. Countless children love creative writing, and some of them even have published books.

Write with integrity and authenticity no matter how much life experience you've had.

If you're young and your world changes somehow, write about that change. Consider the memoirists who write their life story, only to see their lives unfold in new and unexpected directions. Then they write about these new lives too.

Glennon Doyle is the first author who comes to mind here. Do the changes in life invalidate those first books? No, it makes it a preserved artifact, a record of an experienced time and a human capable of growth.

Live a life worth writing about, but resist getting to the end of that life before you put it all down in words.

PHYSICAL LIMITATIONS

Writing is a verb. It's something we *do* with our bodies. But we often forget that, living in our heads while our poor hands, shoulders, arms, back, and neck suffer. We tend not to think of it until the body stops being able to *do*.

For some writers who have unfortunately suffered to a point where these physical effects impede the ability to get the words out (whether it's from writing or something else), a fear is born that they cannot or will not be able to physically write. That they are no longer writers.

Even if your body stops you from getting to the keyboard, you are still a writer.

Technology is your friend and assistant in this.

The solution will obviously depend on the nature of your physical limitation. It might be as simple as a different tilt to the keyboard, switching to a pen and paper, a different chair or no chair at all. Dictation, either with software or another person. Or AI assistance.

There is help.

If you're not there yet but fear a physical limitation in the future (perhaps you already have the niggling warning signs of carpal tunnel syndrome) then make positive changes now before you actually have something to worry about.

Some writers have other physical situations that aren't born out of repetitive overuse injuries. Maybe it's a chronic illness, or a disability of some kind. I cannot speak on this outside of my own experiences with a chronic neurological condition, as every person's body tells a different story. Is there a way, any way, you can tell your story? Just because it might not be able to be done with a pen or a keyboard, could there be another option for you? You have a story to tell. What will it take to get it out?

ISOLATION AND LONELINESS

For many authors, the writing life is a solo act. We sit at our desks alone, living in imagined worlds. Mostly this is a welcome state, an uninterrupted time in our thoughts.

But too much alone time does take its toll, and many authors are negatively affected by the solitude.

Handled right, large amounts of solitary work don't need to end in feelings of isolation and loneliness, so it's nothing to fear. Even for writers who are cowriting, the alone time is a critical part of the creative process for most. So embrace that. But don't make it everything. Just about every mental health modality includes social connection as a critical aspect of a contented, healthy human.

Get up, get out, and connect. It's hard if you're an introvert (especially a Grade A Introvert like myself), but it's not impossible and it's almost always beneficial.

Your family, your friends, your local community. Get amongst them in a way that feels good and right to you. Find writing friends and participate in the writing community. This doesn't have to be extroverted networking at a huge event. A quiet, shy conversation with a fellow author, kicked off with "Hi. What do you write?", can have a remarkable positive effect. Even online connection has its benefits.

It just takes a brief connection with a single person to eliminate loneliness.

FINANCIAL UNCERTAINTY

What if you make some money from your writing sometimes, but it's inconsistent? Unreliable?

Financial uncertainty is a fear for many people in many industries, not just the arts, but it is a particularly ubiquitous one in this field.

Being a writer is not like having a regular job with regular hours and regular pay. You can have that and be a writer at the same time, and many authors do fine in that arrangement.

But if you're dedicated to making your living with your writing alone, overcoming this fear takes a certain amount of acceptance. A stable, regular income is not guaranteed.

Accept that and move on to working, doing everything you can to not only earn the money but be smart about using what money you do earn, so that during the times when income does ebb and flow, it won't automatically mean uncertainty.

BALANCING RESPONSIBILITIES

Writing is likely not the only thing you do.

Even without a day job, writers have other responsibilities. It's an unfortunate fact of the world that if said writer happens to be a woman with children, keeping a household together, those responsibilities are statistically proven to be far more numerous and less visible than the responsibilities of other demographics in our society.

Will I be able to handle being a writer with everything else I have to do?

What if I can't balance everything?

It's a real fear for a lot of us. The fear grows new angles when we try to balance and then falter. Balls get dropped, wheels come off. Guilt comes in. Fear festers and expands.

It's all okay.

The trouble here is not that we can't balance all the demands of life equally. It's that no one can. At least, not in the way our culture wants us to believe we should be doing it. We're told that balance means something that it doesn't.

Think of how a person literally balances on a tightrope.

You walk along in small steps, but you're not keeping everything perfectly in the middle, and you're constantly moving. You lean to one side, then correct to leaning to the other, always edging forward, sometimes quickly, sometimes slowly.

There will be times when you lean into your writing, giving it the most. In those times, the housework might fall behind, the kids might have more screen time (or just have to put up with you closing the door to write). You might not work such long hours in your day job, and you might miss a few social engagements.

There will be times when you're required to lean into other areas of life. Kids get sick, you get sick, the state of the cleanliness of the house starts to be a health risk, you run up against busier periods at work or peak social times like holidays or birthdays. It doesn't mean you can *never* write during these times, it's just that you might not be writing as much. It might be messy and unpredictable, but that's what walking a tightrope can feel like. That's balancing.

Keep shuffling, one step at a time, side to side, ever forward.

BURNOUT

Burnout is different things to different people and has had different names, but we can all generally agree that burnout is a crippling state of exhaustion and depletion following more output than our minds and bodies can cope with.

For writers, burnout is too much thinking, too much writing. It's not enough rest, not enough connection, not enough input from the nonwriting life, if we even remember there is a nonwriting life.

When burnout hits a writer, alongside the usual physical maladies like physical exhaustion and illness, writing is so difficult we might as well call it impossible.

Most people don't fear burnout until they've been in it. Those who have experienced it often fear getting themselves into this state again.

Burnout is one case where we can clearly see fear as a mechanism designed to keep us safe. Burnout is physical as much as it is mental as much as it is emotional and spiritual. It's legitimately dangerous, so it makes sense to be scared of it. But that fear can often stop a writer from working, or working to their potential, for fear of working too hard.

So, do we just work less? Always keep something in the

tank so we're never depleted? That's one approach, and it might serve some well.

Alternatively, you could do what you didn't do that led you to that initial burnout.

Listen to your body. Not your intellect. Don't listen to that part of you that loves writing so much that it's all you want to do. Don't listen to the part of you that strives to achieve against everything in your way. Listen to your actual physical body. Fatigue, pain, foggy thinking, tension, anxiety, anger and other irritable emotions (yes, emotions are a part of the body). Some days your body will be happy to go hard and work until all hours. Other days you will need a slower input mode to rest and rejuvenate. We writers are a naturally intellectual breed, used to obeying and trusting the mind, and that's great in some instances. But in this one, the mind can fool us and lead us to danger. Meanwhile, the body keeps the score.

WRITING CONVENTIONS

Writing conferences, workshops, readings, and all those kinds of writerly gatherings are amazing for so many reasons. They're also absolutely terrifying for so many reasons.

Not all writers are antisocial introverts, but it is definitely a common personality trait in the field. To an antisocial introvert, actively putting yourself in a crowd? Why not just dive into a tank of piranhas? It will amount to the same feeling, but with the plus side that you don't actually have to talk to the piranhas.

Social stuff can be hard. But what's the fear here? It's a fear of being rejected by the group, of being seen as an impostor. It's the fear of looking like a fool. Many of the fears listed in this book will crop up in an ultra-condensed form at a writing conference.

But a gathering of writers is also magical. It can be a balm to all those jangled nerves and lurking fears, a cure for the isolation the writing life can bring, and an opportunity for opportunity in itself.

Maybe you'll meet your future agent. Maybe your new best friend. Perhaps you'll learn something about the craft that will send your book soaring. Maybe you'll hear a marketing tip that rockets you to the top of the charts. Or maybe you'll hear someone speak of a fear you share and you'll feel instantly connected, even if it's from the back of an auditorium.

A gathering of writers is a meeting of souls and minds just like yours. You love writing, everyone else there loves writing. You can't be an impostor in a place where you so clearly belong.

It will get easier, the more events you attend, yet the anticipatory nerves might remain a thing no matter how many writing events you go to.

Suck it up.

There's a value exchange here. The cost is the bad feelings that such events stir up, the fears. The reward is the incredible benefit such events are almost guaranteed to deliver, which in most cases will send those fears packing.

NOT HAVING TIME TO WRITE

There are some aspiring authors (and I use the term "aspiring" very deliberately here) who fear not having enough time to write so much that they don't actually write.

These aspiring authors could be writers, if they chose, but fear of imperfection stops them before they even start.

In this case, it's not the fear of the writing not being perfect. It's the fear of the external writing conditions not being perfect.

Countless writers have written countless books in the slips of time between other facets of their lives. It's pulling a few minutes here or there and getting some words down whenever or however you can.

Other writers are not the sort who can reliably write in this piecemeal approach (me) but still require dedicated sections of time even if they don't have it in huge chunks (also me). For those writers, I assure you that there is a chunk of time in your day. At least one. That chunk doesn't need to be any longer than ten minutes. Five is very short but might work for some. Ten minutes is a few hundred words. By the end of a year, that's more than one hundred thousand words.

Don't let the fear of not having time stop you from seeing

all the time you do have. It might just look different from what you were expecting.

SUCCESS

Fearing success might seem odd to some.

Why on earth would someone fear success?

Because success means living up to a standard you might not be able to replicate. It means a lot of hard work to maintain and potentially even surpass previous success.

If we're counting success here as book sales and engaged readers (which rank somewhere on most authors' versions of success), then success also means a new range of external expectations. Your writing means something to someone out there, so of course you want to keep on serving those people. But can you?

Just keep on writing for the same reasons that brought you to the page in the first place. Keep on telling your stories in the way you want to, and let it be okay if that changes. And let it also be okay that some people won't be okay with this.

Consider also the different elements of success. Yes, royalties and readers are obvious. But what about the successes that no one else can see? The pleasures in turning up to the page. The enjoyment of playing in your wordy worlds. The satisfaction of closing the words for the session in the knowledge that you did your best work and created something new for yourself first. Define your own success and be okay with that definition living in constant flux.

QUALIFICATIONS

What gives me the authority to write this?

What right do I have?

Writing without qualifications, we fear we won't be believed, that we won't be respected or taken seriously. The qualification is the proof that we know what we're talking about, the permission to be a part of the conversation in the first place.

Writing qualifications come in all forms. There are formal degrees, the BAs, the MAs, the MFAs, the PhDs. There are also other institutionalized certifications, the coaching certificates, the teacher trainings, etc.

There are also qualifications that don't come with certificates issued by institutions. The fiction you've already written with no other certifications is a certification in itself. So are the life experiences you've had.

Sure, if you're writing a genre of nonfiction that claims a particular expertise like medicine, you're going to need to have that formal qualification, the proper learning and certifications. That's common sense.

But for most writing, the formal qualification is another

form of permission slip that we don't actually need to make our writing dreams a reality.

Go and get the qualification if you want it. If you feel you need it. If you can afford it.

But remember, as you author your own life, your own learning path, and your own books, that already gives you the permission to write it all down.

Look to your life for the qualification you already have. You might be surprised to learn how much you've learned.

CRITICISM FROM FRIENDS AND FAMILY

What if my family doesn't support my writing?

What if they criticize my efforts?

What if my friends don't like my book?

What if they criticize my author way of life?

We are social creatures, hardwired to go with the crowd, to be accepted and to be loved. So when the people closest to us don't support our efforts, when they criticize our work or our career choices, it truly hurts.

There are two fears going on here: a fear of not being supported and being criticized as a writer, and a fear of the work itself being criticized.

The latter is the easiest to overcome. Don't show your work to anyone in your circle. If they seek it out on their own, then there's nothing you can do about that. Let that control go, let them have their opinion and perhaps ask them to keep it to themselves. I don't even want to know when friends or family have read my work, let alone what they thought of it. If this is the case for you, explain to your people that it's easier for you to get the work done when it feels like no one will read it.

The other fear is trickier. Not having the support of people you love to do something you love can be demoralizing, and it has taken many a would-be writer away from the page, often for good. This feels more like a criticism of you rather than of your actual writing.

But the honest truth is, you don't need anyone's support. Let them have their opinions and keep going.

It might be something that you feel you need to prove to them.

I can be a successful writer!

I am a successful writer!

Let that color your motivations if it feels right to you. But, ultimately, you are the only person who needs that proof. So prove it to yourself first.

Also, consider the different kinds of support someone might offer your writing. It might not look like actively cheering you on to pursue your literary dreams, but the act of simply not impeding your writing can be supportive. Anything they do for you that makes your life easier can be an indirect way of supporting your writing (even if they don't actually know it). Them simply loving you supports your writing.

READING

Writing and reading go together. While there are plenty of readers who don't have writing aspirations, a writer who isn't a reader is a rare creature.

This connection, an insistence that a writer must read, is drilled into us in the most famous pieces of writing advice (you likely already know that Stephen King quote).

But it can all get a bit confusing.

We're told that if we want to publish in a certain genre, we must first read everything in that genre, and we're also told that writers must read widely. Both are valuable pieces of advice, even if they completely contradict one another. If we had all the time to read an entire genre *and* read widely, there wouldn't be time to write.

We're also advised to read analytically. To pick apart the prose and understand how and why it is like it is and why we like it, or don't. Also good advice. But what happens when you find yourself sucked into a story and forget there's even a book in front of you?

As a result, with all this reading advice comes the fear that we're bad readers. That we're not reading enough, or that we're reading the wrong things, or reading in the wrong way.

When children get to independent reading age, parents

are encouraged to let them read whatever they're drawn to. It's good advice, meant to foster a love of reading and take the pressure out of the process.

Writers should be given that same advice.

Read whatever you want, however you want.

Yes, a careful analysis of a text can be a useful study. But how will you know if a book was good enough to draw you in if you were too busy studying it to get drawn in? So, read first and then revisit to study.

Read widely if lots of things appeal to you, but if you only enjoy one type of book, then read that.

Read narrowly if you need to study a genre. This is generally good advice for writers looking to intentionally crack an existing market. For writers following their curiosity and muse, it's likely you're already familiar enough with that genre for it to get your attention, and your curiosity will lead you to read more in that space anyway.

Take the pressure out of it.

Read when it feels good and right. If that's a novel in a day, then read that. If it takes you two months to read a novel, then read that. You write at your own pace, and you can read that way too.

BEING DEVOURED BY A FLESH-EATING VIRUS

This is the only fear in this book that you have no control over. It doesn't come from you, and you cannot control how it affects you and your life. It's the only fear listed in this book that might actually kill you. The rest of the fears in this book are not real, or rather, the threat is only as real as you make it.

It's also the only fear in this book offered with my tongue planted firmly in my cheek. It's a joke.

Oh, flesh-eating viruses are totally real and absolutely terrifying! But the odds of you being attacked by a flesh-eating virus are so low that you might as well not even think about it, accept that it exists in the world and get on with your writing and the rest of your life without that fear stopping you.

As for the rest of the fears in this book, it's okay to get on with your writing, accepting they exist too but moving on regardless.

Don't let your fears stop you from living.

Don't let your fears stop you from writing.

JOIN THE CREATIVE WRITING LIFE

Subscribe to The Creative Writing Life newsletter.

You will receive:

- Inspirational advice for your writing and author life in a monthly email from Kate.
- Free books and other helpful resources for writers.
- Special offers from The Creative Writing Life sponsors.
- Discounts on books and other items.
- Early access to new books and other resources.
- News and other helpful information to help your writing.

To sign up, visit
www.thecreativewritinglife.com/newsletter

ABOUT THE AUTHOR

Kate Krake is the author of fantasy fiction, and personal and creative development for writers.

She is passionate about folklore, pop culture, long distance walking, and curious trivia. She can usually be found with her nose in a book, her ears in a song, and her head in the clouds.

Kate has lived all over Australia and currently lives in Perth, Australia.

Connect
www.katekrake.com
www.thecreativewritinglife.com
www.katekrakefiction.com

kate@thecreativewritinglife.com

ALSO BY KATE KRAKE

FICTION

Night Shift At The Shadow Bay Hotel

Witch Against Wicked

A Maze of Murder

A Mask of Chaos

A Trial of Ghosts

A Wreath of Ruin

A Hex of Wolves

A Trick of Terror

A Coven of Demons

NONFICTION

The Creative Writing Life

Writing Beyond Fear

How To Be A Better Writer

The NaNoWriMo Survival Guide

How To Write Your First Novel

Tarot Writers

Tarot Spreads For Writers

One Word Tarot Meanings

Journal Arcana

Inkwell & Elm publishes premium resources to help writers and other creatives achieve success.

The Inkwell & Elm Group

The Creative Writing Life
www.thecreativewritinglife.com

Tarot Writers
www.tarotwriters.com

Writing Prompt World
www.writingpromptworld.com

www.ingramcontent.com/pod-product-compliance
Lightning Source LLC
Chambersburg PA
CBHW072002290426
44109CB00018B/2100